PUB V

— IN —

Wiltshire

Nick Channer

COUNTRYSIDE BOOKS
NEWBURY BERKSHIRE

First published 1993
This new edition 2007
© Nick Channer, 2007

COUNTRYSIDE BOOKS
3 Catherine Road
Newbury, Berkshire

To view our complete range of books,
please visit us at
www.countrysidebooks.co.uk

ISBN 978 1 84674 049 7

Photographs by the author

Cover picture showing the Wiltshire Downs
on the Tan Hill Way
supplied by Bill Meadows

Maps by Gelder Design & Mapping

Designed by Peter Davies, Nautilus Design
Produced through MRM Associates Ltd., Reading
Typeset by CJWT Solutions, St Helens
Printed by Borcombe SP Ltd., Romsey

Contents

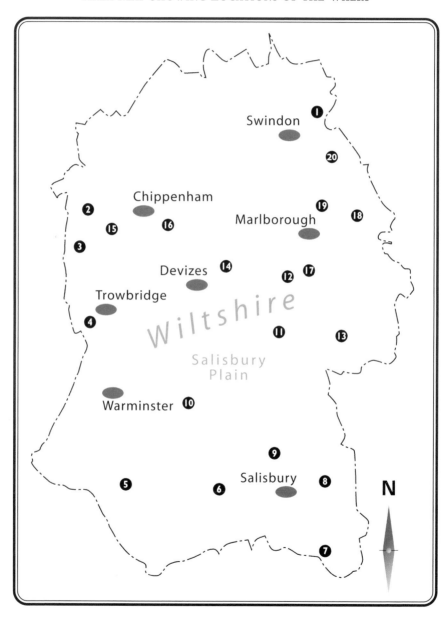

Walk

PUBLISHER'S NOTE

We hope that you obtain considerable enjoyment from this book; great care has been taken in its preparation. However, changes of landlord and actual closures are sadly not uncommon. Likewise, although at the time of publication all routes followed public rights of way or permitted paths, diversion orders can be made and permissions withdrawn.

We cannot of course be held responsible for such diversion orders and any inaccuracies in the text which result from these or any other changes to the routes, nor any damage which might result from walkers trespassing on private property. However, we are anxious that all details covering the walks and the pubs are kept up to date and would therefore welcome information from readers which would be relevant to future editions.

The simple sketch maps that accompany the walks in this book are based on notes made by the author whilst checking out the routes on the ground. However, for the benefit of a proper map, we do recommend that you purchase the relevant Ordnance Survey sheet covering your walk. The Ordnance Survey maps are widely available, especially through booksellers and local newsagents.

INTRODUCTION

Being a fan of country pubs and good beer, I relished the prospect of finding 20 good pubs and 20 good walks to accompany them in this area of infinite variety. I tend to think Wiltshire is underrated as a county. Perhaps too many people speed through it on their way to the West Country, eager to escape the congested environs of London and the pressure of modern-day life. After the clutter of the Thames Valley and the home counties, Wiltshire's stark beauty and spacious landscape inspire a sense of space and freedom, as well as providing a fascinating window on our ancient history.

Apart from the timeless prehistoric sites, the enigmatic monoliths and barrows, the great houses and the sweeping chalk downlands, there are belts of richly-coloured woodlands and forest, snug villages and mellow stone cottages. Various rivers and canals thread their way through Wiltshire and, over the years, they too have played a crucial role in shaping the county's varied scenery.

The walks in this book, all of which are circular and include full route-finding instructions, are designed to offer a wonderful insight into the changing character of the county's rural heartland. There are walks across mysterious Salisbury Plain, in the downland country of north Wiltshire and through the picturesque, unspoiled valleys of the rivers Avon, Marden, Kennet, Nadder and Frome. The By Brook and the Chittern Brook also feature, as does the Kennet & Avon Canal, which is approaching its bi-centenary and survives as a lasting monument to the engineering achievements of the pre-railway era.

All the walks start and finish at a welcoming inn, where walkers will find a range of real ales and appetising pub fare to satisfy those in need of sustenance and refreshment. There are brief details about where to park and information on places of interest within easy reach of the walk route to help you plan a full day out if you wish. Although landlords have given their permission for cars to be left in their car parks whilst their owners are out walking, it is common courtesy to consult the staff before setting out.

You don't have to be a really adventurous hiker with years of experience under your belt to complete these walks. But be prepared for difficult conditions from time to time – even on the shorter routes. Some of the walks cross open, exposed downland, where there is little or no opportunity to shelter from the elements; other routes explore low-lying ground and lush water meadows which can be prone to flooding. Appropriate footwear is always an important consideration when out walking and a small rucksack to carry waterproof clothing is recommended, as is a copy of the relevant Ordnance Survey Explorer map.

Finally, I hope you enjoy these wonderful country walks as much as I did. I believe they reflect the diversity and true spirit of Wiltshire – one of England's loveliest counties. Happy walking.

Nick Channer

ACKNOWLEDGEMENT

My grateful thanks to Brian Reynolds for his hard work and advice during the preparation of this guide.

The Carriers Arms

FROM THE VILLAGE OF SOUTH MARSTON, THE WALK HEADS ACROSS COUNTRY TO ROVES FARM AND ON INTO SLEEPY SEVENHAMPTON BEFORE RETURNING TO THE START ACROSS A LANDSCAPE OF PASTURES AND HEDGEROWS.

When you consider he created one of the world's best-known fictional characters, worked in naval intelligence and travelled widely throughout the world, it may come as something of a surprise to discover that the James Bond novelist Ian Fleming is buried in a quiet churchyard deep in the Wiltshire countryside. Fleming, who died in 1964 at the age of 56, lived at 16th-century Sevenhampton Place, outside Swindon, at the time of his death and his nearby grave marks the halfway point on this very pleasant rural walk.

THE CARRIERS ARMS is an unpretentious village local that is the ideal watering hole on a country ramble. Wadworth 6X and Courage Best will easily satisfy the thirsty walker, and there is a tempting choice of baguettes, jacket potatoes and ploughman's lunches. Main meals also feature on the menu and there is a traditional roast on Sunday. The Carriers Arms is open all day on Saturday and Sunday but closed Monday lunchtime.
☎ 01793 822051

> **How to get there:** South Marston is off the A420, between Swindon and Faringdon. From the M4 leave at junction 15, take the A419 and the A420. Follow the signs for South Marston and the pub will be found in the village centre.
> **Parking:** In the pub car park,
> **Length of the walk:** 5 miles. Map: OS Explorer 170 Abingdon, Wantage & Vale of White Horse (GR 193882).

THE WALK

1 On leaving the **Carriers Arms,** turn left, then left into **Old Vicarage Lane.** Pass **Chapel Lane** and turn left at the war memorial, crossing the stile to the right and following the path parallel to the tarmac lane. Cross a field to the road and turn left. Veer right at the sign for **Nightingale Wood** and walk along to the car park. Turn left, following the sign for **Kestrel Walk** and **Heron Walk.** Keep to the obvious path and pass beneath power cables. As it bends right, branch off left to a hedge gap. Follow the path ahead and on the left are the buildings of **Roves Farm,** a popular family visitor attraction. Pass a sign for the **Maze** and walk through the car park.

2 Turn left and follow the track, with **Sevenhampton Place**

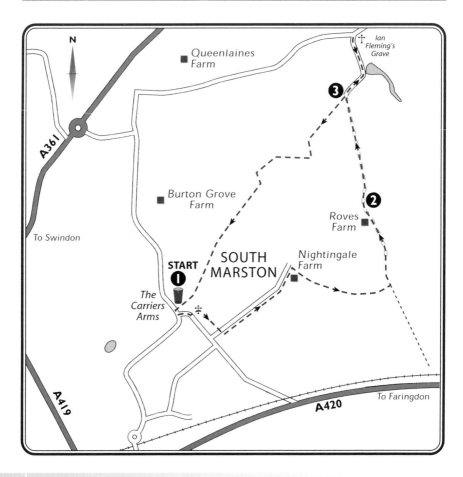

parkland on the right. Turn right at the road for the church – Ian Fleming's grave is on the left as you enter the churchyard. Retrace your steps along the lane, passing a sign for **Roves Farm Visitor Centre.**

3 Go through a galvanised gate on the right to join a waymarked field path and continue in the same direction across farmland. Pass through a gate and over a footbridge before taking the permissive path round the field edge to its far corner. Go left in the adjoining field, crossing a stream, and keep right. Follow the path (part of a heritage trail) along the field edge, beside the stream, and veer off to the left. Keep following the waymarks, skirt a field, with trees on the right, and turn right over a stile before the corner. Turn left in the field, following the green sward round the perimeter, cross a stile and aim slightly left in the pasture to another waymark. Follow the permissive path and turn left at the next waymark, where there is a footbridge and stile. Keep straight ahead towards **South Marston**, ignore a path in the right-hand corner of the field and then cross a paddock followed by a lane. Turn right at the junction, right again at the next T-junction and return to the pub where the walk started.

PLACES OF INTEREST NEARBY

Coate Water Country Park, south-east of Swindon has boats for hire and a coarse fishery day ticket is available. The Ranger Service offers a selection of talks and activities for clubs, societies, community groups and colleges. There is also a programme of walks and events open to everyone throughout the year. Facilities at Coate Water include a café, play area, pitch and putt, orienteering, bird hides, model railway and barbecue hire. For more information call the Ranger Centre on 01793 490150.

The White Hart

T HIS VERY PLEASANT WALK INITIALLY FOLLOWS AN OLD COACH ROAD ALMOST AS FAR AS THE VILLAGE OF NORTH WRAXALL. IT THEN HEADS SOUTH TO CROSS THE DONCOMBE BROOK, A TRIBUTARY OF THE BY BROOK, AT THE POINT WHERE IT RUNS THROUGH PRETTY WOODLAND. A STEADY CLIMB BETWEEN THE TREES IS FOLLOWED BY A LENGTHY SECTION ON THE ROAD, THOUGH BEING A COUNTRY LANE TRAFFIC ALONG HERE IS MERCIFULLY LIGHT. THE LAST STAGE OF THE WALK, BETWEEN THE VILLAGES OF SLAUGHTERFORD AND FORD, COINCIDES WITH A STRETCH OF THE MACMILLAN WAY LONG-DISTANCE TRAIL.

If you think the surroundings on this delightful walk look vaguely familiar, then there's a reason. Much of this corner of Wiltshire was used in the filming of the original 1967 version of Hugh Lofting's classic children's film *Doctor Doolittle*, starring Rex Harrison,

Anthony Newley and Richard Attenborough. Despite the charm of the story, in which the central character talks to animals and travels the world in search of the pink sea snail, and some catchy melodies by songwriter Leslie Bricusse, this big-screen adaptation was never a great success.

THE WHITE HART is a quaint old coaching inn dating back to the 16th century and located directly beside the By Brook. Not surprisingly, given its charm and character, the pub made an appearance in *Doctor Doolittle*, but the fame didn't stop there. In later years the inn's picturesque setting was chosen for a Carlsberg advertisement with foam used to look like snowflakes. Open all day every day, the White Hart offers a good, appetising menu, with the likes of beer-battered cod, sirloin steak, chicken florentine, home-made pie of the day, Aberdeen Angus burger and a variety of lighter meals available. Wadworth 6X and a guest beer feature among the ales.

✆ 01249 783075.

How to get there: From Chippenham follow the A420 road towards Bristol. On reaching Ford, turn left at the sign for the White Hart. Pass the pub on the left, cross the By Brook and turn immediately right into the car park.

Parking: There is a spacious car park by the By Brook, a few yards from the White Hart.

Length of the walk: 5½ miles. Map: OS Explorer 156 Chippenham & Bradford-on-Avon (GR 841746).

THE WALK

① From the car park turn left, immediately crossing the **By Brook**. Pass the **White Hart** and, at the junction just beyond it, cross over to a footpath which climbs between trees to reach the A420 with **Ford church** on your right. Go over to a byway (**Old Coach Road**). Pass between trees, beginning a moderate climb with

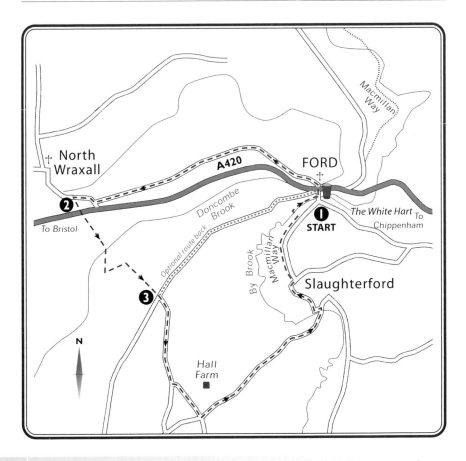

glimpses of **Ford** down below. Pass **Hillside Cottage** and, on reaching the higher ground, continue ahead along a muddy track running between hedgerows. Pass several transmitters on the right of the track and keep ahead to a bungalow. At the road just beyond it, turn right and follow the lane round to the left, passing between trees. Look for a cottage on the right and, just beyond it, step off the road to join a bridleway on the left.

② Climb steadily and walk along through the trees to rejoin the A420. Cross over and take the bridleway down through trees to reach a lock-up garage on the right and a nearby storage tank.

Two paths are seen running ahead through the trees. Take the right-hand path and follow it down to the **Doncombe Brook**. Cross the brook and follow the well-used path up the wooded hillside. If it is very wet and muddy, take the parallel woodland path running along the top of the bank to the left. Farther up, the path swings left at a junction with a 'private' sign seen on the right. Follow the path and soon it merges with another path. Keep ahead, avoid turnings off, and follow the path round to the right. When another path crosses our route, exit from the woods into a field and walk ahead along its left-hand boundary.

3 On reaching the road, you have a choice. The quickest and most direct way back to **Ford** is left along the road. However, traffic here is often heavy and quite fast; to avoid speeding cars and lorries, take the lane opposite and follow it to a junction. Keep left, pass the entrance to **Hall Farm** and turn left at the next intersection. Turn left at the next main junction, pass **Slaughterford church** and then join the **Macmillan Way** on the left. Follow it across fields and meadows beside the **By Brook** and, on reaching a stile, exit to the road. Turn right for **Ford** and right again at the junction for the **White Hart** and the car park.

PLACES OF INTEREST NEARBY

The National Trust village of **Lacock** is one of Wiltshire's most popular visitor attractions – a perfect example of medieval England. These days Lacock is regularly used as a scenic backdrop to period television dramas and films. It featured prominently in the BBC adaptation of Jane Austen's *Pride and Prejudice* in 1996 when it became the fictional home of Elizabeth Bennet and her family. Look out for **Lacock Abbey** which was converted to a house in the 16th century and later became the home of William Henry Fox Talbot, one of the early pioneers of photography.

The Quarryman's Arms

THERE IS A GREAT DEAL OF VARIETY ON THIS DELIGHTFUL HILLY WALK LOCATED IN AN AREA RENOWNED FOR ITS STONE QUARRIES. THERE IS A FLAVOUR OF THE COTSWOLDS ABOUT IT, EVEN A HINT OF THE DERBYSHIRE DALES, WITH ITS ROLLING FIELDS, GLORIOUS WOODLAND, DRYSTONE WALLS AND STONE COTTAGES.

The walk makes for the village of Box, where there are splendid views of Brunel's 2-mile Box Tunnel. The year 2006 marked the bicentenary of the birth of Isambard Kingdom Brunel – the man who quite literally changed the face of Britain. As well as planning the Clifton suspension bridge, he designed the *Great Western* steamship and built docks, railways, tunnels and viaducts. Through his genius, he has left us with a permanent legacy. The last part of the walk follows the banks of the pretty By Brook.

THE QUARRYMAN'S ARMS is hidden away on a hillside above the village of Box. Its position is so out of the way that it's amazing anyone can find it. But find it they most certainly do, and it is particularly popular with walkers and cyclists. Hardly surprising, as the place has a distinctive but genuine atmosphere. The inn is an unusual split-level building. From the outside it looks very small, rather reminiscent of an old fashioned railway station in the days of steam. Inside, it is spacious. In the heyday of the stone industry it became a favourite haunt of quarrymen who worked the quarries in the area. The little snug, situated on the right as you come in, used to be the candlemaker's shop. If you are planning to eat here, then try and get a table near the balcony. The views over the surrounding countryside are stunning. Butcombe and Wadworth 6X are among the real ales, while the appetising menu offers, amongst other fare, Quarryman's platter, burgers, scampi and chips, an all-day breakfast, jacket potatoes and sandwiches.
✆ 01225 743569.

> **How to get there:** Box Hill is immediately to the south of the A4, between Corsham and Bath. From Corsham bear left beyond the Rudlow Park Hotel into Hedgesparrow Lane, then go into Barnetts Hill and right at the fork. The inn is on the right. From Bath and Box turn right into Beech Road, then right at Barnetts Hill.
> **Parking:** The pub has a spacious car park.
> **Length of the walk:** 4 miles. Map: OS Explorer 156 Chippenham & Bradford-on-Avon (GR 834693).

THE WALK

1 From the front of the inn join a waymarked track opposite and follow it past the **Old Post Office** on the left. When the track reaches a T-junction, go forward onto a grassy bank and veer left. Follow the line of the path across the grass to enter the trees. When you reach another junction, turn right and follow the path to the road. Bear right and go down to the road junction. Turn right into **Boxfields Road**. Follow the road between the trees and then veer left to join a waymarked path cutting across the field. When you reach a drystone wall, bear left and follow the path with the wall on your right. After a couple of minutes, swing right, through a gap in the wall, and follow the path towards a line of trees on the far side of the field.

On reaching a track, turn right and follow it as it bends left passing between borders of ornamental trees and shrubs. Pass the main entrance to **Hazlebury Manor** on the right and continue beyond the pond. At this point swing left as the track heads towards open fields. Follow the path down the slope between shrubs and bushes and lines of trees. Pass a pond on the left. At the point where a bridleway crosses our route, go through the stile in front of you and descend the grassy slopes. This part of the walk is a scenic delight, particularly in summer. The semi-wooded slopes offer a network of paths to delight the walker. Follow the path as it enters an area of thickish woodland. You are now on a wide bridleway (usually wet and muddy after rain). Ignore turnings off and two stiles on the left and continue on the main bridleway through the woods, following it down to a road.

2 Turn left on a sharp bend and go up the lane to the junction. Bear right and follow the road, beside some houses. At the junction join the **A365** and follow its pavement into the centre of **Box**. There are good views on the right, across the village. Pass **Chapel Lane**. At the next junction bear sharp right to join the **A4**. Pass the **Bear Inn**, from which Cromwell barred the local

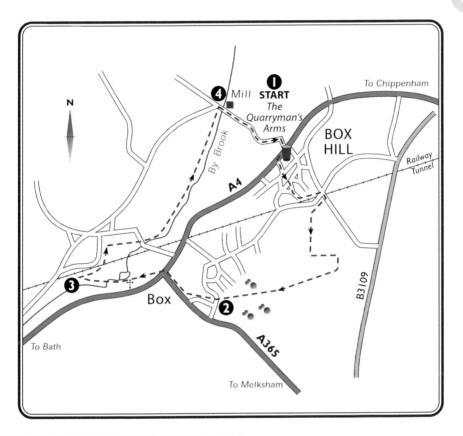

parson on the grounds that 'he is an ignorant and scandalous minister profaning the Sabbath'. Just beyond the inn turn sharp left into **Church Lane**. Follow the lane, passing to the right of the church. At the far end of the lane bear right by **Box House Cottage**, going down the waymarked path between walls and pass over a pretty stream further down. By taking a few steps to the right to a gate you will be treated to a delightful prospect, as here the stream cascades charmingly down beneath the trees.

Resuming the walk, cross the bridge over the **By Brook** and at the junction go forward and straight up towards the left hand edge of the trees. Aim for a gateway beside the trees and continue over the next field. Glancing back at this stage, there are superb views back towards the village of **Box** nestling in the valley below. Away to the west, you can spot traffic zipping along the A4. Further up the hillside there is an impressive view of **Box Tunnel** on the right. Its scale and the classical design of its entrance make it one of Brunel's greatest engineering achievements. It is over 3,000 yards long and was officially opened in 1841. At the time, it was the longest railway tunnel in the world and at one stage there were 4,000 men working on its construction. According to legend, the sun shines through the tunnel on Brunel's birthday in April. At this stage of the route you are walking above a shorter section of tunnel as the line once more cuts through this hillside. The graceful stone parapet above the mouth of the tunnel is just a few yards away to the right of the path.

Continue up the slope towards a gate and stile, veering left just before reaching them, and walk along to a stile in the field corner. The parapet above the western portal of the tunnel can just be seen down on the left. Cross into the next field and follow the hedgerow to a stile by a galvanized gate.

3 Follow an enclosed path to the road and then turn sharp right at the junction (signposted **Hill House Farm**). Pass the farm, then bear right at the gate and stile, crossing the field to the stile in the next boundary.

Cross it and descend the hillside to join the road. Cross over the **By Brook** and then bear immediately left to join a waterside path. Go over the footbridge and turn right. Note the spectacular sluice gate and the racing foaming water over to the right. Follow the clear path over another bridge and when you reach a stile on the left, leave the path and enter the field. Proceed ahead across the water meadows, running parallel with the **By Brook**. In the next boundary pass through the gap into the next field and continue ahead. In the next hedge, with the brook now some way over to the right, go over a stile and follow the right boundary of the field until you exit into the lane.

4 Turn right and after a short distance bear right where a sign says 'unsuitable for motors'. Cross the **By Brook** and go between the buildings of the mill. Follow the lane as it rises quite steeply between hedgerows and banks. A backward glance reveals good views of **Colerne,** a neighbouring village on the horizon. The church stands out proudly on the hilltop. The control tower at the adjacent airfield is also visible. **Colerne** was an RAF station until its closure in the mid 1970s. Eventually, after a stiff climb, you reach the main **A4**. Cross it to join **Hedgesparrow Lane**. After about 50 yards, at the junction, join **Barnetts Hill**, veer right at the fork and follow the road to the inn and car park.

PLACES OF INTEREST NEARBY

If you enjoy nostalgic steam train rides through picturesque countryside, then make a point of visiting the **Avon Valley Railway** at Bitton between Bath and Bristol. Train rides begin at Bitton station and run between Oldland Common and Avon Riverside Station – a round trip of almost 6 miles. Within a short distance of Avon Riverside you can find country walks, a picnic area, pubs and river boat trips. General enquiries 0117 932 5538.

The Poplars

THE WALK CROSSES FARMLAND BEHIND THE POPLARS BEFORE RUNNING ALONG THE BANK OF THE RIVER FROME ON THE WILTSHIRE/SOMERSET BORDER. THE SCENE BY THE RIVER IS QUITE CHARMING. ON THE HILL ABOVE THE RIVER THERE ARE DELIGHTFUL VIEWS ACROSS THE VALE TO SOMERSET. THE RETURN LEG IS A PLEASANT STROLL ACROSS FARMLAND.

Wingfield is a scattered village, much of which is set back from the main B3109 Bradford-on-Avon road down several narrow lanes well hidden from passing traffic. North of the village, though not on the actual route of the walk, is Midway Manor, once the home of General Shrapnel, the 18th-century inventor of the exploding projectile of the same name.

THE POPLARS has been a pub since the early 1950s. Prior to that it was an off-licence and village shop. The whitewashed building is more than 250 years old and was originally a farmhouse. The Poplars is a quintessential English pub with all the right ingredients. But there is something else that sets it apart from the rest. The inn has its own cricket ground, an innovation introduced by a previous landlord. During the cricket season the Poplars can become extremely busy when teams and supporters gather in the lounge and public bars to celebrate and commiserate.

Real ales include Wadworth 6X and Henrys IPA. The menu includes cod, chips and mushy peas, lambs' liver and bacon, and stuffed peppers with vegetable risotto. For lighter fare there is a choice of jacket potatoes, as well as pâté and ploughman's lunches. The Googly-filled bap is one of the pub's great favourites.

✆ 01225 752426.

How to get there: Wingfield is several miles west of Trowbridge, just to the south of the A366. Join the B3109, following the signs for Wingfield. The Poplars is on the right coming from the direction of Trowbridge or Bradford-on-Avon.

Parking: There is room to park at the Poplars. Wingfield village centre is on the other side of the main B3109. There is limited parking in Church Lane, particularly in the vicinity of the church.

Length of the walk: 3¾ miles. Map: OS Explorer 143 Warminster & Trowbridge (GR 822567).

THE WALK

1) From the pub car park turn left and follow the narrow lane running alongside some cottages. When the lane peters out, go forward onto a drive as waymarked. Follow it to the right of a private garage and continue on along a path between fields. At the next stile, on the right, cross over and bear left. Cross several

fields via stiles and make for the road. Bear left and follow the lane with a line of cottages and houses on the right. As you begin to approach some farm buildings, cross the right hand boundary into the field. The path is waymarked. Turn left and follow the field edge, with farm buildings on the left. Keep to the path and follow it to a footbridge in the field boundary. Cross it and then head for a stile in the opposite boundary.

Walk ahead in the next field, making for the top right corner where there is a stile. Follow the track between trees to reach some water meadows. Cross them and over to the right is the fast-flowing **river Frome**. The river, a tributary of the **Avon**, represents the county boundary between Wiltshire and Somerset. In time a charming old cottage comes into view over on the Somerset bank, its gardens running down to the water's edge. Rising above it are the houses of **Tellisford**, a village prettily situated only just within the borders of Somerset. Look for a galvanised gate ahead beside an old footbridge.

② The scene here is most picturesque, and it is worth breaking off from the walk for a few moments in order to stand on the bridge and gaze at the river upstream and down.

Returning to the walk, go up **Vagg's Hill** away from the Somerset border, noting a right of way on the right to **Rode**. Pass a house, then follow the tarmac lane between banks of trees and bushes. The lane is steep in places. Further on, the lane levels out and in a right-hand gateway there are splendid views over to Somerset on the far side of the valley. Pass a footpath on the left and continue. On the right is a turning to **Langham Farm**. On the left is woodland.

Pass several private properties on the right, and then a farm. The road veers slightly left and soon cuts between fields and hedgerows before reaching the junction. Cross over into **Poplar Tree Lane**, noting the Somerset border along to the right. Pass **Dillybrook Cottage** on the right and continue along the road. Glancing back across the fields, there are good views of the trees soaring above the **river Frome**. Walk past some cottages and

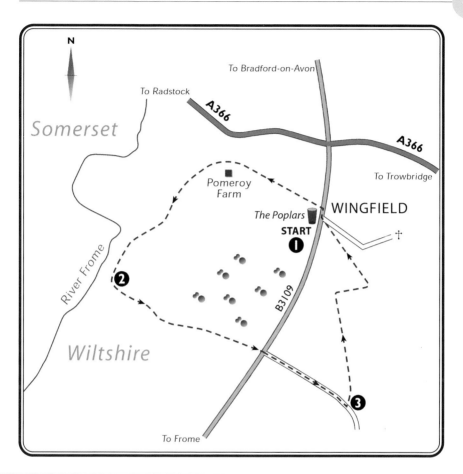

when the road veers right, turn sharp left to join a bridleway to **Wingfield**.

3 Follow the broad bridleway as it runs between hedgerows, trees and bushes. There are fields either side of the way. Further on, the bridleway narrows to a path. Eventually, you reach a junction. Bear right, still on the bridleway. All around you are good views over farmland.

As the bridleway swings right, within sight of a farm, turn left over a stile in the hedge and enter the field. Follow the right-hand boundary into the corner, and then in the next corner, where there is a footbridge, cross into the next field. Proceed ahead to the far boundary and join a grassy path beside the garden of a private house. Pass several houses and follow the track as far as the **B3109 road**. At the junction turn right and walk along the verge and then the pavement. **Church Lane** on the right, leading to **Wingfield church** and the village centre, is worth exploring. Returning to the **B3109**, cross it and return to the **Poplars** car park.

PLACES OF INTEREST NEARBY

The **Chippenham Museum and Heritage Centre** offers the chance to journey through time. As well as enjoying various exhibitions and special events, you can learn about Chippenham through the Saxon, Georgian and Victorian periods, and discover the effect the Civil War and the Second World War had on this Wiltshire town. Telephone: 01249 705020.

The Seymour Arms

THE WALK MEANDERS ROUND THE VILLAGE BOUNDARIES FOR A WHILE BEFORE PASSING THROUGH SEVERAL CHARMING HAMLETS ON ITS WAY TO THE TOP OF WINDMILL HILL. FROM HERE THERE ARE SUPERB VIEWS OVER THE BLACKMOOR VALE. THERE ARE SEVERAL SECTIONS OF ROAD WALKING, ALONG QUIET COUNTRY LANES.

———— •◦• ————

East Knoyle is a large scattered village on a greensand ridge surrounded by fine walking country. Christopher Wren, whose father was rector at East Knoyle, was born in a room above the village shop in October 1632.

THE SEYMOUR ARMS is 17th-century and is named after the Seymour family who once owned part of the village. During the summer, the walls of the pub are covered with Virginia creeper. Until recent years, this historic building shook to the sound of traffic thundering by on the main A350 road at the front of the pub. However, the much-needed East Knoyle bypass, completed in 1996, has restored a sense of calm to the village street. Accommodation is also available, with two double rooms.

This is a Wadworth house and the real ales include Wadworth 6X and Henry's IPA. Sandwiches, ciabattas and other snacks are available, and there is also an à la carte menu and a traditional roast on Sunday. Please note that no food is served on Sunday evening and the pub is closed on Mondays. The pub has a pleasant beer garden. Dogs are welcome.

Ø 01747 830374.

How to get there: The Seymour Arms is off the A350 East Knoyle bypass between Warminster and Shaftesbury. Follow the signs for the village and the inn is in the main street, at the southern end of East Knoyle.

Parking: There is a car park at the Seymour Arms. Alternatively, there should be room to park in the road by the church, or close to Wren's shop and post office.

Length of the walk: 4 miles. Maps: OS Explorer 143 Warminster & Trowbridge and OS Explorer 118 Shaftesbury & Cranbourne Chase (GR 882302).

THE WALK

1 Take the waymarked path at the back of the pub, crossing a stile by a gate and then across the field towards the bypass. Over to the left are very good views of **East Knoyle**, with the church tower visible among the trees on the hillside and groups of cottages gathered in higgledy-piggledy fashion around it. Cross another stile, descend a flight of steps to the road and go over to

Millbrook Lane. Turn left after several yards and follow the waymarked path parallel to the bypass for about 100 yards. Go through a gate and bear right. Pass a pond and walk to a junction with a grassy path. Cross the stile and head slightly left in the field to the next stile. Pass through a plantation, cross a stile and turn left with the fence on the left. Join a muddy path running beneath the trees. Pass under a stone bridge built by the original owners of nearby **Clouds House** as part of a carriage drive.

The path descends quite steeply under the trees and there is a field on the right fringed by woodland. Soon the path widens to a track before reaching the road. Turn left and follow the road between hedgerows. Pass **Park Farm** and when you reach the **East Knoyle bypass,** cross over and go through a wrought-iron kissing-gate. Follow the path to another gate in the top right corner of the field, noting a small enclosure containing a sapling beneath which is the inscription: '1992 – in memory of Mum and Dad'. Cross a drive leading to **Clouds House** and join a waymarked path, continuing ahead across a paddock with the grounds of **Clouds House** on the left. This was built for the Wyndham family in 1886, but burnt to the ground soon afterwards. 'Clouds', appropriately named in view of its hilltop position, was completely rebuilt in 1893.

2 When you reach a stile leading you out to the road, bear left and follow the lane between high hedges and trees down to some charming stone houses at the junction. Turn left and at the next junction, near a telephone box, keep right. This is **Milton**, a peaceful hamlet of houses and cottages. When the houses peter out, swing left over a stile and then bear right, up the field. Looking back, on these grassy slopes, there is a delightful vista of **Milton** with steeply rising wooded hills beyond. It is a picture so typically English in both beauty and character that it could almost come straight from the pages of a calendar or the lid of a biscuit tin.

Pass through the gap into the next field, climbing steeply.

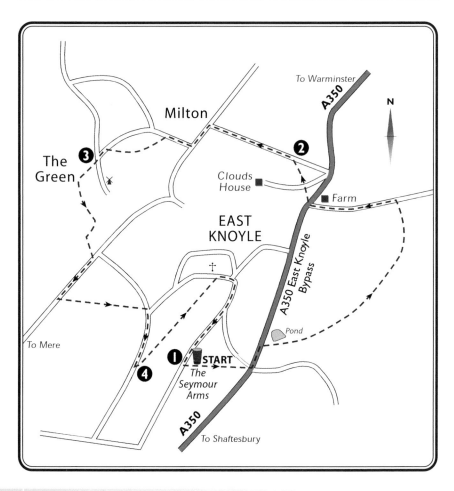

When the ground levels out, proceed ahead to the far boundary and go out to the road. Turn left and follow the lane down to the T-junction at **The Green,** another tiny settlement on the outskirts of **East Knoyle.**

3 Bear right for a few yards and then left opposite the **Fox and Hounds** where there is a striking view across the **Blackmoor Vale.** Head across the grass, keeping the view on the right. Follow the path between lines of trees and scrub. Ignore a branch path to the right and continue ahead on the higher path. Further on, there is a major junction, with a path on the right, a path straight ahead and a path veering to the left. Take the left route and follow it over a wooded plateau, continuing to swing left. Ignore the sunken path below. Between the trees on the right are magnificent and memorable views of the **Blackmoor Vale** – a vast green patchwork stretching to the horizon.

Soon the trees thin to reveal even more spectacular views. You are now on top of **Windmill Hill,** 650 ft above sea level. If time permits, you may like to continue to the road in order to look at the old stone windmill on the opposite side. Retrace your steps along the path towards the **Fox and Hounds** for a short distance. As you approach the point where the trees on the left begin to obscure the views, veer over to the left and look for a thin bridle path cutting down the bank. This is so narrow and restricted in places you wonder how on earth a horse could negotiate such a hazardous passage. The views are constant and unchanging as you make your way down to the road at **Underhill.**

Turn right and follow the road towards **Mere.** Some way down you reach **Hartmoor Farm.** Bear left just before it through a kissing-gate to join a waymarked path running alongside some paddocks. Pass a lake on the right. Walk to a gate, bear left down the field to the next two gates, climb steeply in the next field to a stile and a line of trees, and veer left at the waymark. Approach a large double fronted house. Head for the drive, turn left and make for the road at **Holloway.** At the junction bear right opposite **The Old Rectory.** After a few yards bear right into **Holloway Lane,** signposted 'Semley and Shaftesbury'. There are various houses and fields on the right and a sizeable area of woodland on the left. When the road bends right, swing sharp left into a field.

4 Head across the open field towards the houses of **East Knoyle,** keeping the woodland on the left at all times. Gradually, the field tapers, the houses of the village growing ever nearer. Go

through a gate into a paddock with the church easily seen through a splendid vista. Join a hard path and continue to the road opposite the church. Glancing back as you reach the gate reveals an impressive view of **East Knoyle** with the hills circling the village like protective guardians.

Turn right and go along to the junction in the village centre. A plaque commemorating Christopher Wren's birthplace can be seen here. His family occupied the premises at the time of his birth as there had been a fire at the rectory.

The land on the far side of the road was purchased by the people of the village in 1975 as an open space for exercise and recreation. Bear right at the junction and walk down the main street of the village. The **Seymour Arms** comes into view further on along the street.

PLACES OF INTEREST NEARBY

The landscaped gardens at **Stourhead,** owned by the National Trust, are among the finest in the country. The lakes, temples, shrubs and rare trees feature in countless books, calendars and postcards. The Palladian mansion was built in the 1720s and the estate also includes Alfred's Tower, a famous folly built in 1772. Telephone: 01747 841152.

BARFORD ST MARTIN

The Barford Inn

M Y ABIDING MEMORY OF THIS SPLENDID WALK IS THE EXTRAORDINARILY ISOLATED TRACT OF WOODED COUNTRYSIDE TO THE NORTH OF THE VILLAGE OF BARFORD ST MARTIN. IT IS DIFFICULT ENOUGH THESE DAYS TO ESCAPE THE CONSTANT REMINDERS OF THE STRESSFUL 21ST CENTURY, AND THE EVER ENCROACHING CONGESTION OF THE SOUTH OF ENGLAND, BUT TO MY MIND THIS WALK MANAGES TO TRANSPORT THE COUNTRY LOVER TO A SECRET UNDISTURBED WORLD OF SILENT WOODLAND AND QUIET PATHS. ONLY AN OCCASIONAL MILITARY HELICOPTER DISTURBS THE CALM. IT IS TAILOR-MADE FOR THOSE WHO WANT TO GET AWAY FROM IT ALL.

On 29th May each year, Oak Apple Day, an old custom, which is associated with pre-Christian tree worship, permits villagers from nearby Great Wishford to gather fallen and dead wood from Grovely Wood. Originally, this tradition extended to other villages, Barford St Martin among them. The custom still includes a ritual ceremony which involves villagers processing to Salisbury Cathedral where, at the steps of the high altar, they proclaim their rights, chanting 'Grovely! Grovely! And all Grovely! Unity is strength'.

THE BARFORD INN used to be called the Green Dragon, and during the Second World War, the Wiltshire Yeomanry dedicated a tank to the pub. Built as a coaching inn and brewery which served pubs within an 8-mile radius up until about the end of the 19th century, the Barford Inn is situated in the heart of the village, on a corner of the A30.

The menu includes a choice of ciabattas, chargrilled medallions of beef and seafood linguini. The real ale on handpump is Dorset Best and Tanglefoot.

✆ 01722 742242.

How to get there: Barford St Martin is a pleasant village lying on a sharp bend of the A30. From Salisbury follow the signs for Wilton and then continue along the A30 to reach the village. The Barford Inn is on the right on the bend.

Parking: There is a huge car park at the rear of the Barford Inn. Alternatively, you could park outside the church, near the junction of Factory Lane and Duck Lane.

Length of the walk: 5½ miles. Map: OS Explorer 130 Salisbury & Stonehenge (GR 056314).

THE WALK

1 From the car park turn right to the junction. Avoid the busy **A30** and bear left along the '**No Through Road**'. Pass through the railway arch and continue with farm buildings on the right.

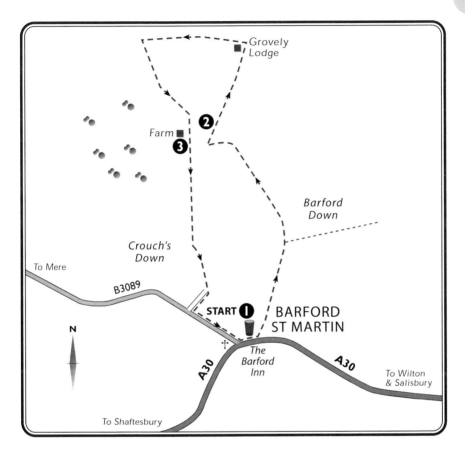

Follow the lane round several bends, avoiding a bridleway on the right. Proceed along the main track as the surface becomes rougher underfoot. Quite quickly you arrive at a junction of tracks. Turn right and follow the bridleway as it cuts deeper into this remote lonely country. The track continues an upward pull, and looking behind you to the south there are impressive views over rolling downland. Follow the track into **Grovely Wood**. At a junction keep right and follow the track between trees.

2 On reaching the next junction, with fields opposite, bear right. Pass **Grovely Lodge** and, at the junction beyond it, turn left.

Follow the track for about ½ mile, then swing left at a path and soon you reach a junction of tracks. Take the left turning and follow it just inside the woodland, with fields over to the left. Continue for some time and eventually you come to a derelict house on the right. Just beyond it join a track and maintain the same direction. After a few paces join another track, keep **Grovely Farm** on the right and, at a triangle of grass, veer right and keep the farm on your right.

3 Keep right at the next fork, a few paces further on, and follow the path along the extreme right edge of the wood. On reaching a field corner, avoid the track running off to the right and look for a tall waymark post. Go diagonally right down the field slope, cross a track and continue between fields. The path heads down towards the **Nadder valley**, gradually becoming more sunken. Either side of you are banks of grass and scrub. Further down, on the northern outskirts of **Barford St Martin**, a housing estate comes into view. When you reach the houses, go down to join **Dairy Road**. Pass through the railway arch and at the junction bear left to follow the **B3089** through the village. The **Nadder** runs parallel to the road, just a few yards away. Note **Mill House** on the right, with the sight and sound of the spectacular thundering mill race capturing the attention for a few moments. Pass the village school and the church. Beyond them is the **Barford Inn** on the left.

PLACES OF INTEREST NEARBY

Originally a 9th-century nunnery, **Wilton House**, near Salisbury, includes Inigo Jones state rooms, a renowned art collection, modern interpretative displays and 21 acres of landscaped parkland. Telephone: 01722 746729.

The King's Head

ON THE CHALK DOWNS ABOVE REDLYNCH THERE ARE WIDE, UNINTERRUPTED VIEWS OVER THE AVON VALLEY AND NORTH TO THE SPIRE OF SALISBURY CATHEDRAL. THE WALK EXPLORES THIS REMOTE DOWNLAND COUNTRY, AND FOR THE NATURALIST THERE IS PLENTY TO SEE, INCLUDING WILD CHALK-LOVING FLOWERS AND PRESERVED HEDGEROWS.

◆●◆

Redlynch is part of a chain of residential communities running along the northern edge of the New Forest and straddling the Wiltshire/Hampshire border. Only a mile away is the Newhouse, a

Jacobean, brick-built 'Trinity' house with two Georgian wings dating from the early 17th century. The house includes a costume collection and various relics associated with Nelson. Also nearby is the hamlet of Lover, which traditionally becomes the focus of attention annually on St Valentine's Day. Scores of romantics flood the village post office with cards and messages to ensure that they are postmarked 'Lover'.

THE KING'S HEAD is 17th-century and very much a traditional country pub. Inside, there are some quaint old features, including beams and low ceilings. In an age when the future of the village inn is under threat, it is good to know that the landlords have worked hard at maintaining the success of this popular hostelry.

The extensive and constantly changing menu caters for most tastes and includes light snacks and more substantial dishes. There is a strong emphasis on local produce, main meals are freshly cooked, and there is choice of two traditional roasts. Among the real ales are Ringwood best bitter and Wadworth 6X. Children are permitted in the large beer garden.
✆ 01725 510420.

How to get there: Redlynch is south of Salisbury, between the A338 and A36. At Downton join the B3080 and at Morgan's Vale bear left into Redlynch. The inn is on the left.
Parking: Apart from the car park at the King's Head, there are a few spaces near the pub or in the vicinity of Morgan's Vale.
Length of the walk: 4¼ miles. Maps: OS Explorer 130 Salisbury & Stonehenge and OS Explorer 131 Romsey & Andover (GR 202213).

THE WALK

① Leave the car park and turn immediately right, following the quiet lane (not to be confused with the road leading up to join the B3080 at **Morgan's Vale**). The lane climbs up beside farmland. When you reach a triangular road junction, swing left and at the next junction veer right where there is a path opposite cutting between hedgerows. At this stage of the walk there are good views over towards the **Avon valley** and beyond. Pass a 'No Through Road' sign followed by several houses and bungalows. There are catkins along this stretch of the route in spring, and a sign indicating the verge is protected. Pass fields on the left and continue along the track as it curves to the right. Over to the west the good views are constant.

Soon the track becomes rougher and muddier underfoot as you begin to climb up the slope. From the top there are splendid views in all directions. Carry on down between the trees which thin somewhat as you approach the buildings of **Barford Down Farm**.

2 Beyond the farm you join the road on a bend. Continue ahead along the road as it cuts across farmland. Note the westerly views. When you reach an isolated whitened brick dwelling on the left of the road, take the track on the extreme right. Climb uphill, with far-reaching views in all directions and, just beyond the track running in from **Pepperbox Hill**, pass through a gate and then bear right as you approach **Privett Farm**.

3 Head down the chalky track noting the views on the right over to the south-west. In the banks along here grows a chalk-loving flower known as dog's mercury. Pass a crosstrack and continue between lines of trees and hedgerows. When the track bends left, continue straight ahead, with good views to the right.

When you reach a junction of tracks, continue ahead and follow the track as it begins to curve left between hedgerows. It runs alongside farm buildings, followed by the entrance to **Templeman's Old Farmhouse**. The track graduates to a lane at this point. Follow its firm surface until you reach a left turning

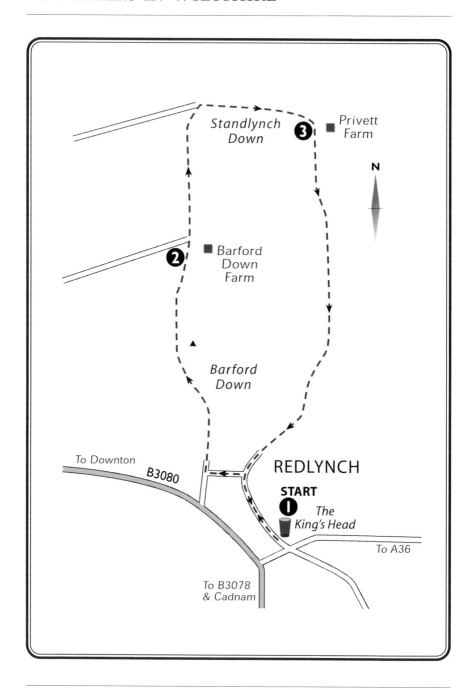

after several minutes. You will probably recognise this route from the earlier stages of the walk. Take the turning and follow the lane back to the **King's Head**.

PLACES OF INTEREST NEARBY

Braemore House, south of Downton, is a splendid Elizabethan manor house containing fine artefacts acquired by ten generations. It was purchased in 1748 by the king's physician, Sir Edward Hulse, and remains in the family today. There was a fire in 1856, ruining the interior but the exterior has remained the same as when it was built in 1583. Telephone: 01725 512468.

The Silver Plough

There is a strong sense of the past and of ancient history on this glorious woodland walk in the countryside to the east of Salisbury. The woods outside Pitton provided timber for the village's waggon-building and wheelwright industries. The contrasting open stretches reveal glimpses of Wiltshire's downland country and close by are the remains of a royal palace which started life as a Saxon hunting lodge.

◆◆

Built during the 12th century, Pitton's St Peter's church dates back to before Salisbury Cathedral, though virtually nothing remains of the original building. The present Grade II listed church was extensively restored in the late 1880s, the exterior rendered with a flint and greensand dressing. Inside you can see an octagonal oak pulpit, as well as a memorial brass plaque commemorating the Zouche family who owned the village during the reign of Charles I.

THE SILVER PLOUGH was converted from a farmhouse around 60 years ago. It has many of the characteristics of a classic country pub: beams, Toby jugs and board games. Dishes available at lunchtime and in the evening might include half a roast shoulder of lamb with mint and garlic gravy, and red bream filled with caramelised onions, prosciutto and pesto sauce. Among the real ales are Badger Tanglefoot and Gold King & Barnes Sussex.
☎ 01722 712266.

How to get there: Follow the A30 north-east from Salisbury towards Andover and turn right for Pitton before reaching the junction with the A343.
Parking: In the pub car park.
Length of the walk: 2½ miles. Map: OS Explorer 131 Romsey & Andover (GR 213132).

THE WALK

1 From the pub, follow the road linking **Pitton** and **Farley** towards the village centre and turn right into the **High Street**. The parish church is on the left. From **St Peter's**, cross the road and follow the path beside the bus stop. Walk along it beside trees, fencing and a hedgerow. On the left are several barns. Pass the recreation ground and, at the next road, cross over to take the path up the bank and through the trees, climbing steeply here between fencing, hedging and rough pasture. From this lofty ground there are very good views over the village of **Pitton** and the downland surrounding it. The church is also seen nestling

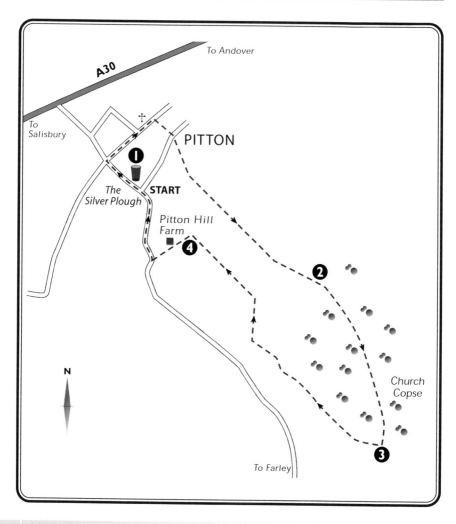

among the trees. Cross two stiles and continue, with a field boundary over on the right. Head for a track leading to **Hale Farm,** cross over and maintain the same direction, following a track now as it runs alongside trees and bushes. Pass beneath the boughs of oak trees along this stretch before a curtain of woodland provides the backdrop. The track narrows to a path and passes by trees, bushes and light woodland.

2 Cross a stile and follow the obvious path as it veers to the right through the woods. Eventually the path joins a clear track and on the left here is **Church Copse**. Keep right at this point and pass a turning on the right, followed by a path on the left. Head for a prominent intersection and turn right over a stile.

3 Ignore the path running diagonally across the pasture and keep the wood on your right. Skirt the trees to arrive at a stile and follow a path – often overgrown in summer – for about 40 yards to a second stile. Continue ahead, following the path inside the woodland at this stage and pass under telegraph wires. On reaching a field, keep ahead with the perimeter on your left. Cross into the next field and aim diagonally right to reach the corner of the pasture. Skirt the field with the boundary on your left.

4 Make for a farm access track, turn left and walk beside farm outbuildings. Head for the road, turn right and look out for the rather striking chalk cliff on the right. Descend the hill into **Pitton** and return to the **Silver Plough**, which will be found on the right.

PLACES OF INTEREST NEARBY

Salisbury, south-west of Pitton, is one of Britain's loveliest and most historic cities. With its assortment of visitor attractions and soaring cathedral spire immortalised by Constable in his famous painting, a walking tour of this ancient settlement is highly recommended. Look out for **Malmesbury House** which Handel used for his recitals and where Charles II stayed at the time of the Great Plague. Contact the tourist information centre on 01722 334956.

The Wheatsheaf

WITH THE SUN SPARKLING ON THE AVON, BATHING THE WATER MEADOWS AND THE ENTIRE VALLEY IN A WARM GOLDEN GLOW, LOWER WOODFORD'S UNSPOILT RURAL SETTING HAS TO BE ONE OF THE LOVELIEST IN THE WHOLE OF WILTSHIRE. APPROPRIATELY, THE ONLY REAL WAY TO EXPLORE THE VALLEY AND APPRECIATE ITS GENTLE BEAUTY IS TO GO ON FOOT. THE WALK EXPLORES THE WINDSWEPT DOWNLAND SLOPES TO THE EAST OF THE AVON BEFORE DESCENDING TO LITTLE DURNFORD MANOR. THE ESTATE IS ONE OF THE FINEST IN THE AREA. FROM HERE THE ROUTE IS ACROSS THE FIELDS BACK TO LOWER WOODFORD.

The village of Lower Woodford is part of an agricultural district heavily populated with tenant farmers and landowners. William

LOWER WOODFORD – *The Wheatsheaf*

Cobbett came this way in 1826 and, remarking on the plight of the farm labourer, he expressed his 'deep shame as an Englishman, at beholding the general extreme poverty of those who cause this vale to produce such quantities of food and raiment.'

THE WHEATSHEAF, which was completely refurbished in 2002, was once a farm and what are now the dining rooms used to be the stables and barns. Various rustic artefacts characterising those pioneering days of agricultural husbandry remain. Beer was brewed here until the beginning of the 20th century. Naturally, the inn has changed significantly over the years and today it is a thriving and friendly country pub with a good reputation for cask conditioned beers and cuisine, with the accent being very much on food. In summer you can eat and drink in the beer garden.

The food, which is available all day, includes sandwiches, jacket potatoes, baguettes and a range of main meals. There is a traditional roast on Sunday. Real ale enthusiasts won't be disappointed either. The choice includes Tanglefoot and a weekly guest beer. Families are very welcome and children can join you in the dining area.
✆ 01722 782203.

How to get there: Lower Woodford is north of Salisbury, between the A360 and the A345. From Amesbury follow the road south through the Avon valley. From the south you can go through Wilton or Old Sarum to reach the village.
Parking: There is usually plenty of room at the Wheatsheaf, and limited spaces in the main street of Lower Woodford.
Length of the walk: 3 miles. Map: OS Explorer 130 Salisbury & Stonehenge (GR 124348).

THE WALK

1 From the car park turn left and pass the front of the inn. Proceed along the main street of the village, which includes various flint and brick cottages and some chalk cob walls. Soon after a

telephone box on the right, you will see a footpath sign. Turn right into the drive of a private house, veering left immediately. Pass the front door of the house and continue ahead to join a path which crosses the **Avon** at a particularly scenic reach of the wide river. Not far from this spot are **Heale House and gardens**. Charles II sought refuge here after the Battle of Worcester in 1651. It was from the house that he set out to visit **Stonehenge**.

Follow the tarmac path and further up there are glorious views back across the **Avon valley** and the wooded downs beyond. Head up towards a farm and some cottages. At the road bear left for a few yards, then right at **Salterton Farm**. Take the bridle track running up the hill to the left of the outbuildings.

② Follow it round to the right and after about 120 yards, turn right through a gate to join a path cutting along the right edge of the field. Follow the grassy strip with delightful views of the valley and **Lower Woodford** nestling beside the clear river and the pretty water meadows. Eventually you reach the field corner. Go through a metal gate, at once crossing the route of a bridleway, and continue along the waymarked footpath through a copse. Beyond it head out over open ground on the higher slopes of the valley. Follow the broad grassy ride as it descends towards some trees. Pass alongside an isolated thatched cottage and bear right just beyond it to join a quiet lane running between rows of trees. Further on, there is more extensive woodland on the right. Stay on the lane to reach a junction.

③ Cross the road and go through a wooden panelled gate marked 'Footpath'. Follow the tarmac drive with a low flint wall and hedge on the right. Above the hedge can be glimpsed the lovely old manor house at **Little Durnford**. The house was the subject of a book called *A Wiltshire Home*, written by a member of the Devenish family, who lived there as a child in the 20th century.

During late winter clusters of snowdrops are often visible over among the trees and shrubs to the right of the drive. As you approach some cottages and a stable block, veer right by a petrol

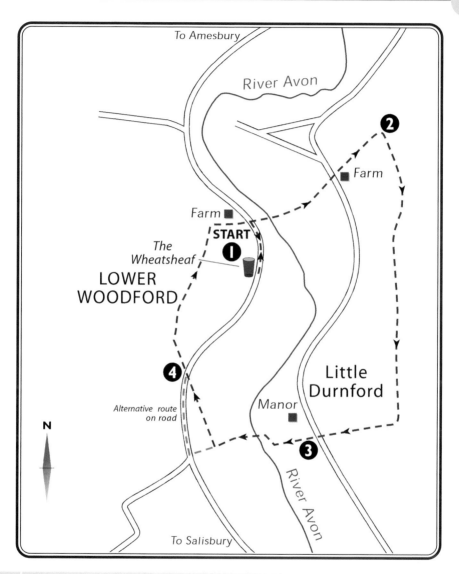

pump and follow the drive towards the stone bridge over the **Avon**. If you look behind you at this stage, you will be able to spot the main house across the extensive lawns. At the second bridge take the path on the right. Walk across the pasture with the brook on your left. At the next bridge cross over to a stile, then cross two further stiles in the right boundary and walk along the left edge of the field. The brook is now on your right. Soon you reach a stile and gate on the left. Pass over it to join a wooded track running to the road. (If there is any problem over access in these fields, follow the main drive to the road and then bear right. Follow the road as it runs past the entrance to 'The Bays' and then take a waymarked path in the left bank.)

4 Cross over to the signposted path. In the field turn right. Keep the road over to the right, pass into the next field and then head diagonally across it towards woodland. As you proceed towards it, join a path running along a field edge with the trees on the immediate right. Farm buildings are visible in the distance. The houses of **Lower Woodford** come into view on the right. Cross a stile and continue towards the farm. Cross the next stile by a gate and make for some cottages to the right of the farm buildings. There are good views on the right of **Lower Woodford** sheltering in the valley. At the farm gate turn right and go down the hill to the junction. Bear right and follow the road back to the inn car park.

PLACES OF INTEREST NEARBY

Heale House Gardens and Plant Centre near Great Durnford comprise 8 acres of magnificent gardens in a formal setting of mellow stonework and clipped hedges. There are delightful walks here through the different seasons, and many of the unusual plants found growing in the garden can be bought in the specialist plant centre. Heale House is well known in Wiltshire for sheltering Charles II after the Battle of Worcester in 1651. Telephone: 01722 782504.

The King's Head

THE WALK PROVES MOST EFFECTIVELY THAT THERE ARE A NUMBER OF RIGHTS OF WAY CRISS-CROSSING SALISBURY PLAIN, PROVIDING ACCESS, ALBEIT LIMITED, TO THIS AUSTERE LANDSCAPE. HOWEVER, THE ROUTE IS OPEN AND EXPOSED WITH FEW OPPORTUNITIES TO SHELTER FROM THE WIND AND RAIN. WHEN WEATHER CONDITIONS ARE NOT AS GOOD AS THEY COULD BE, IT IS A WALK IDEALLY SUITED PERHAPS TO THE MORE ADVENTUROUS RAMBLER, BUT ON A SUNNY SPRING DAY, THE SURROUNDINGS ARE NEVER LESS THAN SPECTACULAR.

When you think of the Plain the image that comes to mind tends to be of an undulating chalk plateau, a hostile, desolate place with much evidence of military activity and a tangible air of ancient mystery. Salisbury Plain and the whole of North Wessex were once the most heavily populated areas in the country, inhabited by the people of the late Stone Age and Bronze Age. Ironically, today, in this overcrowded island of ours, the Plain is one of the loneliest and least populated tracts of land in the south of England, if not all of Britain.

Situated on Salisbury Plain, and once very much a traditional village pub, the **KING'S HEAD** is now a chain hostelry. From the outside it is rather a rambling old stone building, internally, however, it is very different with modern décor and a minimalist style of design. Baguettes, ploughman's, salads, gammon, egg & chips, a traditional roast on Sunday, and many other dishes are available. Beers include Wadworth 6X and Butcombe bitter. No food is served on Sunday evening, and the pub is closed on Monday.
Ø 01985 850269.

How to get there: Chitterne lies on the southern edge of Salisbury Plain, on the B390 Heytesbury to Shrewton road. It is in remote country, the nearest town of any size being Warminster. The inn is at the western end of the village.
Parking: There is a car park at the King's Head, or you may find space to park in the vicinity of Chitterne church.
Length of the walk: 6 miles. Map: OS Explorer 143 Warminster & Trowbridge (GR 988438).

THE WALK

1 From the front of the **King's Head** turn right and follow the road, with the **Chitterne Brook** in the fields over on the left. The brook is a 'winter bourne'. Dry in summer, the channel runs through the centre of the village. Pass some farm buildings on the right. Where the road bends left, turn right to join a waymarked path running between trees and bushes. This is part of the **Imber Range Perimeter Path**, a 30-mile circular walk

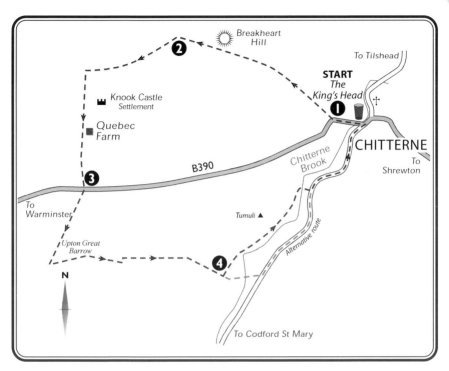

following the outer boundary of the military firing and training area.

Follow the sunken bridleway and, when the trees thin out, there are views over fields either side of the route. Glancing back at intervals reveals magnificent far-reaching views across the southern edge of the Plain. The views to the south are the best, as you gaze out over a wide landscape of open chalk downland, dotted with belts of woodland, stretching down to the **Wylye valley**. On these grassy slopes the only sounds you are likely to hear are the booms and bangs of the army, and perhaps a skylark swooping overhead.

Pass over a crosstrack and continue. Go through a small copse and keep to the grassy track. As you head over **Breakheart Hill**, you will see the **MOD ranges** on the right. It is important to keep to the **Imber Range Path,** ensuring that you do not trespass beyond the warning notices. After you have crossed the military road, you will reach a junction of paths.

2 Veer left and continue along the **Imber Range Path**. Avoid a turning down to a small copse enclosing some farm buildings and continue up the slope to another junction where there is a byway on the left. This is the start of the next stage of the walk. At this point you are leaving the **Imber Range Path**. However, on a clear day it is worth continuing along the track for some time until it begins to descend the slope. At this point, 600 ft above sea level, you can see a range of distant rounded hills, including **Cotley Hill, Battlesbury Hill** and **Scratchbury Hill**. There are good views to the north across the heart of **Salisbury Plain**. The 360° views from here are so extensive that when visibility is good you can probably see up to 15 miles or more. Beside the path there are the remains of various barrows and tumuli.

Return to the byway and follow it in a southerly direction towards some farm buildings, re-crossing the military road. On the left of the track is visible evidence of **Knook Castle** and its ancient remains. The old ramparts and ditches are now little more than just lumpy grassy mounds. Pass the farm and continue down to the **B390 Chitterne–Heytesbury road**.

3 Cross the road to a byway. Follow it with light woodland on the left. There are spectacular views to the west towards **Heytesbury**, where the First World War poet Siegfried Sassoon lived until his death in 1967, having earlier been stationed locally. Pass a corrugated barn and after about 120 yards swing left through a metal hand gate to join a waymarked byway. On the left among the trees is the outline of **Upton Great Barrow**. This homeward stretch of the walk is over civilian-owned land, the army ranges being to the north of the **B390**. When the track bends left, continue ahead along the left boundary of a field in the corner. Go through a hand gate and turn left for a few yards to a waymarked bridleway. Following the reassuring waymark, turn right and follow the bridleway across the field, which may have crops. Continue and, on the opposite side, pass through another gate. Keep ahead, commencing a slow descent and always keeping the boundary fence on your left.

Go through further gates and continue to a field corner where you will follow the path as it swings right, following the field edge to a final hand gate on your left. Go through and head down a farm track with a line of fir trees on the right to reach a metalled track.

At this point, an alternative route would be along the bridleway across fields to the road back to the start.

④ For the main route, turn left and follow the track. The scenery changes quite significantly in character as the landscape becomes softer and less severe than the bare downland of earlier. Go along the track until it bends left at a gate. Leave the track at this point and follow the waymarked path across the field to a gate. Pass through it and keep to the right boundary of a large field. Eventually you reach a stile on the right. Cross the stile, go over a footbridge and continue to the road. Bear left and walk back to the **King's Head** in the village.

PLACES OF INTEREST NEARBY

Stonehenge is a World Heritage Site of unique importance and interest, surrounded by the remains of ceremonial and domestic structures. The site is to the west of Amesbury, at the junction of the A344 and the A303. Telephone: 01980 624715.

The Ship

THE SCENERY OFFERED BY THIS WALK IS SURELY SOME OF THE FINEST TO BE FOUND ANYWHERE WITHIN THE BOUNDARIES OF WILTSHIRE. THERE IS A SPLENDID MIXTURE OF HIGH EXPOSED DOWNLAND PROVIDING STUNNING VIEWS TO THE VALE OF PEWSEY AND BEYOND AND, DURING THE LATTER STAGES OF THE WALK, GENTLE SHELTERED COUNTRYSIDE AROUND THE WATER MEADOWS AT THE HEAD OF THE AVON VALLEY.

⬩•⬩

Until around the beginning of the 19th century, there was a bustling market at Upavon. The meeting point of two important routes also helped to bring trade to the village, and to establish Upavon as a vital and prosperous community between the towns of Andover,

Marlborough and Devizes. Not surprisingly, the old market square is still the focal point. As well as the restored church with its castellated tower and octagonal Norman font, there are a number of picturesque old buildings worth closer inspection.

With its thatched roof and sturdy beams, the **SHIP** is one of the quaintest pubs in the area and one of the prettiest buildings in Upavon. There is plenty to tempt the hungry walker inside, with steak and ale pie, scampi, sirloin steak and venison burger among a good selection of dishes. For something lighter, choose from a range of filled baguettes and baps. There is a traditional roast on Sunday. Wadworth 6X features among the real ales.
Ø 01980 630313.

How to get there: The Ship is at the heart of Upavon. The village lies at the junction of the A342 and the A345, between Marlborough and Salisbury.
Parking: Limited spaces at the front of the pub or park on the road nearby.
Length of the walk: 4¼ miles. Map: OS Explorer 130 Salisbury & Stonehenge (GR 134549).

THE WALK

1. On leaving the pub turn left and then immediately left and walk along the village street to the junction with the A342 Andover road. Turn left, pass the parish church and the reading room on the left and make for a right-hand bend by **The Pottery**. Avoid the right turn here and go straight on along a footpath running between houses. Shortly it becomes a sunken path which climbs gradually between trees and margins of vegetation. Along here you get a taste of what is to come as swathes of sweeping downland edge into view in the distance. Emerge from the trees and continue across open ground. Away to the right are the buildings of **RAF Upavon**. Keep to the left of a golf course and

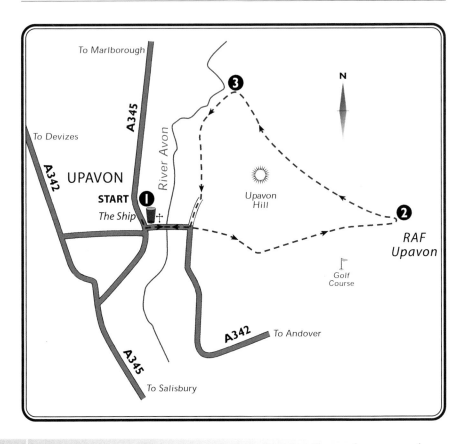

make for the club's north-east perimeter. Drop down gently to a track and turn left.

2 Away on the horizon is the chalk outline of the **White Horse** at **Alton Barnes**. Follow the chalk track – grassy in places – and when it bends right to a 'No thoroughfare, private road' sign, keep ahead on the track. Pass beside rows of trees and begin a gradual descent, following the track beside belts of woodland.

3 Head for a T-junction with trees beyond and turn left. Keep the woodland on your right and follow the path as it runs parallel with the A345. Pass between hedges and keep in line with power cables as you begin the walk's homeward leg. At this stage the **River Avon** peeps into view over to the right. Merge with a track on the outskirts of **Upavon,** pass some outbuildings and keep an eye out for **Upavon** across the meadows and farmland. On reaching a bridleway sign and a barn, continue ahead and soon the track becomes a tarmac lane. Pass some houses on the left and, at the road, keep right and return to the village centre. At the main road, turn right, then right again to reach the **Ship.**

PLACES OF INTEREST NEARBY

The delightful town of **Marlborough** is close by and perfect for shopping, exploring on foot or relaxing over a civilised afternoon tea at the renowned award-winning Polly Tearooms. As well as visiting the shops and the church, you can discover a veritable rabbit warren of passages and alleyways behind the handsome shop fronts and half-timbered buildings of the High Street. Telephone: 01672 513989

The White Hart

THIS GLORIOUS RAMBLE AT OARE, SOUTH OF MARLBOROUGH, HAS TO BE ONE OF WILTSHIRE'S LOVELIEST WALKS. WITH ITS STRETCH OF CANAL, REMOTE HAMLETS AND VIEWS OVER SPECTACULAR OPEN DOWNLAND, THE ROUTE INCORPORATES MANY OF THE COUNTY'S MOST FAMOUS FEATURES AND CHARACTERISTICS. FROM OARE THE WALK HEADS WEST ACROSS ISOLATED TERRAIN TO THE TINY VILLAGE OF HUISH BEFORE FOLLOWING QUIET COUNTRY LANES FOR SEVERAL MILES. AFTER A STRETCH BY THE KENNET & AVON CANAL, THE LAST LEG OFFERS WONDERFUL VIEWS OF THE 822-FT GIANT'S GRAVE ON THE HORIZON.

The churchyard at Huish includes the grave of David Niven's first wife Primula whose family lived opposite the entrance. The couple were married here before departing for Hollywood, where Niven soon established himself as an actor of international renown. Primula died tragically in 1946 at their Los Angeles home following a fall and was buried in this peaceful churchyard overlooking glorious swathes of Wiltshire downland. She was 28 years of age.

THE WHITE HART is a typical example of a simple, unspoilt rural inn. Popular with ramblers following the nearby Kennet & Avon Canal towpath or exploring the scenic country of east Wiltshire, the pub offers a friendly atmosphere and a cosy bar. Expect a range of baguettes, soup, scampi and chips and traditional Sunday roast among other fare. Beers include Ramsbury, Butts, and Wadworth 6X. The White Hart is not open on Monday.
✆ 01672 562273.

How to get there: From Marlborough follow the A345 south towards Pewsey and Salisbury. Look for the White Hart on the right when reaching the village of Oare.
Parking: In the pub car park.
Length of the walk: 6 miles. Map: OS Explorer 157 Marlborough & Savernake Forest (GR 157632).

THE WALK

1. From the pub turn right and follow the main road. Bear right into **Rudge Lane,** head for the edge of **Oare** and follow the lane round to the left. Soon you reach a bridleway and adjoining footpath on the right. Head for outbuildings and stables and make for a gate and stile. Cross over onto a track and skirt a field to reach a gate down in the bottom left corner. Turn right for several paces to another stile, avoiding the bridleway running off to the left. Cross the field, passing to the right of woodland, and make for a gate. Cross a path to another stile and follow the direction of the waymark. Avoid a footpath sign over to the right and go down to the bottom boundary of the field to reach

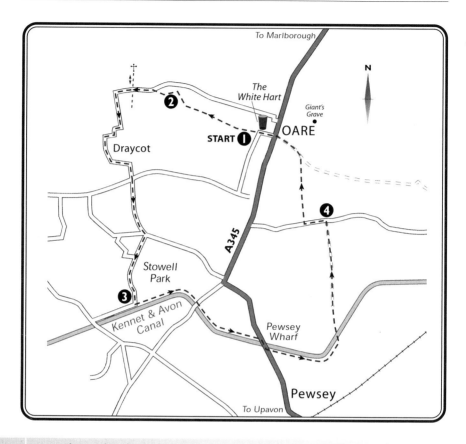

a stile and galvanised gate set amidst trees. Follow it down to a lane and turn left.

2 Walk through the hamlet of **Huish** and look for the church standing up on the hillside to the right. Walk up to **St Nicholas's church** and then retrace your steps into **Huish**, turning right at the T-junction. Follow the lane and look back for a delightful view of the settlement set against the towering escarpment. Walk along to **Draycot Farm** at **Fitz Payne** and continue on the road. Look for **Huish church** in the distance across the fields. Aim for a road junction and keep ahead for **East Stowell** and **Pewsey**. Pass another lane on the right further on and turn right at the

junction just beyond it. Ignore the drive to **East Stowell Farm** and continue to the point where the road sweeps round to the right.

3 Join the canal towpath by the entrance to **Cannings Cottage** and turn left for **Pewsey Wharf**. Pass beneath a dilapidated pedestrian bridge and look for **Stowell Park** to the left. At the next bridge cross over to follow the opposite bank and head for **Pewsey Wharf**. On reaching the buildings, continue with the canal on your left and follow the towpath as it begins a gradual left bend. Ignore a stile on the right and continue. On reaching bridge 113, pass beneath it and then turn immediately right. Cross the bridge and follow the track ahead between fields. The **Giant's Grave** is seen on the horizon. This hilltop site is chiefly associated with a charming legend claiming that anyone who runs along the top of this unchambered long barrow seven times will wake the sleeping giant.

4 At the road turn left and pass a bungalow. About 50 yards beyond it, where a right of way crosses the road, turn right and proceed up the left side of the field. Look for an exit in the top corner, turn left and follow the bridleway between hedges. The surface graduates to tarmac as you reach the outskirts of **Oare**. This is **Pound Lane**. At the main road turn right and return to the pub.

PLACES OF INTEREST NEARBY

Knap Hill, to the north-west of Pewsey, is one of Wiltshire's lesser-known treasures and the site of a four-acre Neolithic causewayed camp dating back to around 2,760 BC. Nearby are the charming villages of **Alton Barnes** and **Alton Priors**. Alton is Anglo-Saxon for 'farm or village by the springs.' The springs can be seen very clearly bubbling away on the bed of a pretty stream near the church of All Saints. The Alton Barnes White Horse was cut in 1812 and can be seen on the hillside.

The Shears

THIS IS SURELY ONE OF THE MOST ISOLATED WALKS IN WILTSHIRE. APART FROM OCCASIONAL SIGNS OF WILDLIFE, YOU WILL PROBABLY HAVE THIS ENTIRE STRETCH OF COUNTRYSIDE TO YOURSELF. IF YOU ENJOY SILENCE AND COMPLETE ISOLATION, THEN THIS GLORIOUS WOODLAND RAMBLE IS FOR YOU.

Nearby Collingbourne Ducis was once held by the Duchy of Lancaster and during the 13th century it belonged to the family of William de Valence, who also held Swindon. For years the village was regarded as too small and too unimportant to play any useful role so it tended to be overlooked by the rest of the world. It was really the dawn of the railway era and the development of the modern road network that put Collingbourne Ducis on the map.

THE SHEARS is one of the best-known pubs in this eastern corner of Wiltshire and very much a local landmark. Dating back to the 16th century and renowned for its thatched roof, the Shears used to be a shearing shed for sheep bound for market at nearby Weyhill – hence its name. Sandwiches, salads and jacket potatoes are among the inn's lighter fare, while fresh seafood specials have helped make the menu one of the pub's more popular features. Brakspear's bitter and a guest beer feature among the real ales. Outside is a small garden area with picnic tables.
✆ 01264 850304.

How to get there: Follow the A338 south of Marlborough and branch off at Collingbourne Ducis, heading east for Cadley. The Shears is situated by a junction.
Parking: In the pub car park.
Length of the walk: 4½ miles. Map: OS Explorer 131 Romsey & Andover (GR 254537).

THE WALK

1 From the pub car park, turn left and walk along the 'no through road.' Several houses are seen along this stretch as you follow the tarmac. Continue ahead, pass a byway sign and a bridleway sign and keep going for a further 60 yards or so to reach a fork. Veer right at this point, follow the byway and begin a moderate climb with impressive views away to the left. Continue climbing with the track bordered by a hedge and bushes on the right and fencing on the left. Pass beside a gate on the left and ignore a bridleway on the right before heading out over high ground. Rows of trees line the route, and carpets of bracken in summer. Pass another bridleway on the left and keep ahead on the byway.

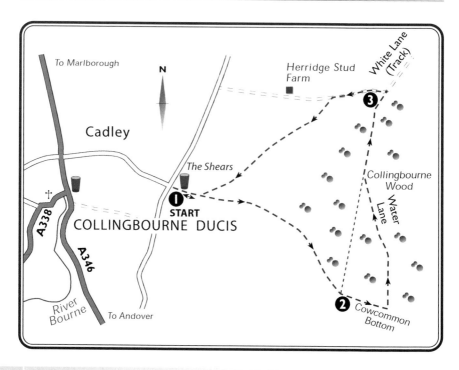

Here and there you'll spot fields between the trees and soon the walk skirts the edge of sprawling **Collingbourne Wood,** managed by Forest Enterprise. Keep ahead with trees to the left and fields over on the right.

2 On reaching the next junction, with **Blackmore Lane** on the right and a bridleway on the left, continue ahead along a broad track. This is known as **Cowcommon Bottom.** Away to the right is an area of extensive beech woodland with lines of trees disappearing into the distance. Take the first bridleway on the left – **Water Lane** – and stay on it as it cuts through mixed woodland. Pass over a cross track and eventually the bridleway curves a little to the left. There is a steady climb through the woodland before you reach an intersection. Continue ahead as the track curves right, pass a track on the left running off into **Whittle Copse** and when **Water Lane** curves right again, look for a bridleway running in from the left to merge with the main route. Keep ahead and then turn sharp left beyond the trees, just after a sign for **Collingbourne Wood**. This is **White Lane**.

3 Descend the slope and keep in line with power cables along here. Pass a bridleway on the left and continue on the byway as it passes rows of beech trees. Ignore a track on the right as you reach the end of the woodland and continue for a short distance between pastures. Turn left just before a steep hill to follow a bridleway, keeping fencing on your left. The track swings to the right and beyond some trees it cuts between fields and grassy slopes to reach a gate. Beyond it retrace your steps back to the pub on the outskirts of **Collingbourne Ducis**.

PLACES OF INTEREST NEARBY

Andover, some 9 miles south-east of Collingbourne Ducis, has the popular **Andover Museum** and the **Museum of the Iron Age,** offering a fascinating glimpse into the mysterious world of archaeology. The museum also tells the story of nearby Danebury Hill Iron Age Fort, another popular visitor attraction in the area. Telephone: 01264 366283.

The Crown Inn

Tʜɪs ᴍᴀɢɴɪꜰɪᴄᴇɴᴛ ᴡᴀʟᴋ ꜰᴏʟʟᴏᴡs ᴀ sᴇᴄᴛɪᴏɴ ᴏꜰ ᴛʜᴇ Kᴇɴɴᴇᴛ & Aᴠᴏɴ Cᴀɴᴀʟ ʙᴇꜰᴏʀᴇ ʜᴇᴀᴅɪɴɢ ᴀᴄʀᴏss ᴡɪʟᴅ, ᴏᴘᴇɴ ᴅᴏᴡɴʟᴀɴᴅ ᴛᴏ ʀᴇᴀᴄʜ ᴛʜᴇ ʀᴏᴜᴛᴇ ᴏꜰ ᴛʜᴇ Wᴀɴsᴅʏᴋᴇ, ᴀ ʟɪɴᴇᴀʀ ᴇᴀʀᴛʜᴡᴏʀᴋ ᴘʀᴏʙᴀʙʟʏ ᴄᴏɴsᴛʀᴜᴄᴛᴇᴅ ʙʏ ᴛʜᴇ Bʀɪᴛᴏɴs ᴀs ᴀ ʟɪɴᴇ ᴏꜰ ᴅᴇꜰᴇɴᴄᴇ ᴀɢᴀɪɴsᴛ ᴛʜᴇ Sᴀxᴏɴs. Tʜᴇ Bʀɪᴛᴏɴs ʟɪᴠᴇᴅ sᴏᴜᴛʜ ᴏꜰ ᴛʜᴇ ʟɪɴᴇ, ᴛʜᴇ Sᴀxᴏɴs ᴛᴏ ᴛʜᴇ ɴᴏʀᴛʜ ᴏꜰ ɪᴛ. Tʜᴇ ʟᴀsᴛ sᴛᴀɢᴇ ᴏꜰ ᴛʜᴇ ᴡᴀʟᴋ ɪs ᴍᴏʀᴇ sʜᴇʟᴛᴇʀᴇᴅ, ᴄʀᴏssɪɴɢ ʟᴏᴡ-ʟʏɪɴɢ ꜰɪᴇʟᴅs ᴀɴᴅ ᴍᴇᴀᴅᴏᴡs ᴏɴ ᴛʜᴇ ʀᴇᴛᴜʀɴ ᴛᴏ Bɪsʜᴏᴘs Cᴀɴɴɪɴɢs.

❖◆❖

The village of Bishops Cannings is probably best known for the legend of the Wiltshire Moonrakers. It is said that when discovered raking the local pond for smuggled liquor casks, several of the locals duped the excisemen into believing they were catching the moon's reflection – or moon-raking. As a result of this charming story, anyone born in the county became known as a Moonraker. The village's most famous landmark is its enormous 13th-century cruciform church, known as the 'Cathedral' of the Vale of Pewsey.

THE CROWN INN has been refurbished in recent times and has a warm, inviting feel. Among a variety of dishes on the menu, you'll find ham, egg and chips; beef lasagne; curry; spicy tomato pasta; pizza; and a range of sandwiches and jacket potatoes. On Sunday there is a traditional carvery. The ever-popular Wadworth 6X is one of the beers on offer.
☎ 01380 860218.

How to get there: Take the A361 from Avebury south towards Devizes and turn right at the sign for Bishops Cannings. Follow the road into the village, pass the church and then turn left into the car park of the Crown Inn.
Parking: There is a car park adjacent to the inn.
Length of the walk: 6 miles. Map: OS Explorer 157 Marlborough & Savernake Forest (GR 037641).

THE WALK

1 From the pub turn right and walk through the adjoining churchyard, keeping to the right of the church. Exit on the far side and turn right at the road. Walk along to a bend and ahead is a gate and a sign for **Court Farm**. Go through the adjacent kissing-gate and along the concrete track, signposted to **Horton**, following it beside trees and out between fields. When the way dwindles to a rough track, keep ahead across farmland and soon you reach the **Kennet & Avon Canal**. Cross it via the swing bridge and turn left to join the towpath. Glance back at this point for a memorable view of the spire of **Bishops Cannings' church**. Follow the canal for some considerable distance, cutting between fields and lines of trees. As you approach bridge

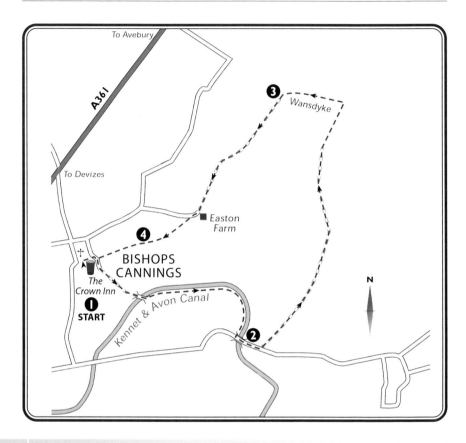

number 132, go up the bank to a gate leading out to the road and turn left.

2 Pass the entrance to **Canal Cottage** and just beyond it, also on the right, are the remains of a war-time pillbox. Keep ahead for several minutes and then turn left at the footpath sign, by the entrance to **Harepath House**. Follow the concrete track and ahead on the horizon is the outline of the **Wansdyke**. Veer left at the fork and climb steadily up the hillside and along to a gate and stile. Continue along the grassy track, following it down to the corner of the field. As the track continues ahead between fences, go through the first of two galvanised gates on the left

and follow the path across the ramparts of the **Wansdyke**. The 14-mile trail runs from **Marlborough** to **Morgans Hill**, near **Calne**.

3 On reaching the next track, turn left, leaving the route of the **Wansdyke** which runs straight on. Pass beside cow sheds and head south. **Bishops Cannings** can be seen down in the **Vale of Pewsey** on the next stretch of the walk, the village dominated by its quintessential Wiltshire setting. Drop down the track to the buildings of **Easton Farm** and join the road at a U-bend. Turn right for several steps, then left at the stile for **Bishops Cannings**. Go diagonally across the field, keeping to the right of a brick house with a slate roof, and make for a stile. Cross over and walk ahead, keeping the field boundary fence on the left. Head for a stile and footbridge in the corner, cross a narrow, elongated pasture to the next footbridge and turn right to skirt the field.

4 On reaching several thatched cottages and a sign for the **Kennet & Avon Canal**, take the path in the general direction of **Bishops Cannings church**. Pass beneath telephone wires, cross another footbridge and continue on the grassy path towards the houses of the village. Cross the next stile and follow a tarmac drive along to the road. Cross over and take the path to the churchyard. Walk through it and return to the pub.

PLACES OF INTEREST NEARBY

The **Kennet & Avon Canal Museum** in Devizes can be contacted on 01380 721279 for details of opening times. The **Devizes Visitor Centre** in the Market Square is well worth a visit, tracing the story of a town steeped in history and legend. Telephone: 01380 729408. The **Wiltshire Heritage Museum** in Long Street includes prehistoric collections of international renown from local landmark sites. Telephone: 01380 727369.

The Flemish Weaver

THE BEAUTY AND GRACE OF WILTSHIRE'S PARKLAND IS PERFECTLY CAPTURED ON THIS WALK, WHICH STARTS IN THE CENTRE OF CORSHAM AND SOON HEADS OUT OF TOWN INTO CORSHAM PARK, LAID OUT BY 'CAPABILITY' BROWN. THIS IS CORSHAM'S GREEN LUNG, WITH ITS PLEASING ACRES AND LAKE VIEWS. THE WALK FOLLOWS SEVERAL QUIET ROADS BEFORE RETURNING TO CORSHAM PARK ON THE HOMEWARD LEG.

With its charming weavers' cottages, mellow-stone period buildings and historic almshouses, Corsham is one of Wiltshire's prettiest towns. At the heart of Corsham stands the fine church of St Bartholomew, which dates back to the 12th and 15th centuries and can be seen at different points on the walk. In the churchyard is the grave of Sarah Jones, who died in 1753 at the grand old age of 107 – a remarkable achievement in those days.

The **FLEMISH WEAVER** is an ideal watering hole for walkers. Food is prepared and cooked in-house and appetising lunchtime dishes include ham, egg and chips, and a range of salads and baguettes. On Sunday there is even a choice of two traditional roasts. Other options might include smoked haddock, cauliflower and broccoli cheese bake, free-range gammon steak, and grilled mackerel fillets. No food is available on Sunday evening. There is always a choice of real ales at the Flemish Weaver, including Bath Gem and Hopback GFB, plus a guest beer.

☎ 01249 701929

How to get there: Follow the A4 west of Chippenham and turn off at the sign for Corsham. Use either of the two car parks located on the left as you enter the town. Walk through the shopping area to the High Street, turn left and head for the pub, situated on the left beyond the tourist information centre.
Parking: The Flemish Weaver does not have a car park. There are two main car parks, both fee-paying, in the centre of Corsham.
Length of the walk: 4 miles. Map: OS Explorer 156 Chippenham & Bradford-on-Avon (GR 873705).

THE WALK

1 From the pub cross the road and head for **St Bartholmew's church. Corsham Court** can be seen on the left. As you approach the church, turn right to a gate and follow a tree-lined avenue for a short distance. Turn left onto a concrete path, go through another gate and walk ahead across **Corsham Park**, aiming to the right of **Corsham Lake**. Merge with an obvious path and follow it as it runs along the right-hand boundary of the

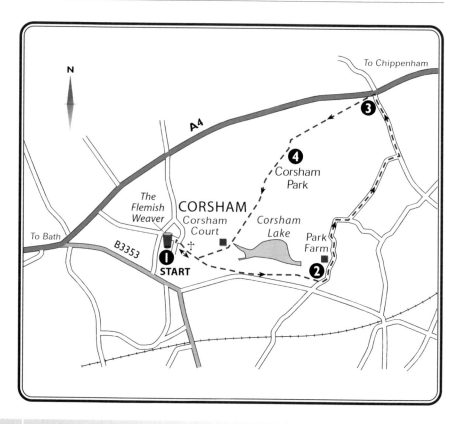

parkland. Look back along this stretch for a superb view of **Corsham Court** and the parish church. Keep parallel with the lake and make for a gate and stile. Cross a track to join an enclosed path running to a field and cross it to a stile leading out to a lane.

2 Turn left, pass **Park Farm** and continue along the road. Soon you are in the depths of the countryside, surrounded by sprawling farmland and a network of hedgerows. Follow the lane round a right-hand bend and keep left at the fork. At the next junction turn left along the road, passing a remote stone-built house on the right. One of **Corsham Court's** imposing entrances can be seen on the left as you approach the A4.

3 Turn left at the junction to pass through a galvanised kissing-gate. Follow the footpath, heading diagonally across parkland. A broad curtain of trees is seen over to the left. After some minutes go through a gate and continue across the parkland; along this stretch look for a wooden gate and an adjoining wrought-iron gate among the trees. Pass through the latter gate, cross a stone bridge and go through a gate to reach a sign 'Please keep to footpath'.

4 Bear right to a stile and maintain the same direction across **Corsham Park. Corsham Lake,** seen in the early stages of the walk, edges into view. Pass a footpath sign and keep alongside a hedge and ditch to reach the field corner. Go through another kissing-gate, obscured by trees and bushes, and follow the boundary to the next gate. **Corsham Court** and **St Bartholomew's church** are clearly seen on this stretch. Keep the ha-ha on your right and follow the path along to the churchyard. Enter it and then retrace your steps back to the pub.

PLACES OF INTEREST NEARBY

Corsham Court is well worth a look. This Elizabethan mansion dates back to 1582 and was acquired by Paul Methuen in 1745 to house his family's collection of 16th- and 17th-century Italian and Flemish Master paintings and statuary. In recent years Corsham Court was used as one of the locations for the film *The Remains of the Day.* The house and gardens are open from 2 pm until 5.30 pm every day except Monday and Friday (but including Bank Holidays) between March and September. Telephone: 01249 701610.

The Soho Inn

THIS FINE WALK BEGINS BY FOLLOWING A STRETCH OF PAVEMENT BESIDE THE A4 – NECESSARY TO REACH THE ROUTE OF THE DISUSED RAILWAY AT BLACK DOG HALT. BEYOND THE OLD TRACK BED, THE ROUTE RUNS BESIDE THE RIVER MARDEN AND THE WILTS AND BERKS CANAL ON ITS WAY INTO CALNE, CONVENIENTLY LOCATED FOR A COFFEE BREAK AND PERHAPS A VISIT TO THE TOURIST INFORMATION CENTRE. FROM THE TOWN, THE WALK QUICKLY MAKES FOR BOWOOD PARK, ONE OF THE KEY FEATURES OF THIS DELIGHTFULLY VARIED RAMBLE. MUCH OF THE SECOND HALF OF THE WALK RUNS THROUGH THIS CLASSICALLY ENGLISH PARKLAND WHICH IS PERFECT FOR EXPLORING ON FOOT IN ANY SEASON.

STUDLEY – *The Soho Inn*

STUDLEY – *The Soho Inn*

The seat of the Marquess of Lansdown, Bowood House lies in 1,000 acres of splendid parkland and woods. The gardens were laid out by 'Capability' Brown in 1763 and a surviving wing of the house was copied from Diocletian's palace in the old Yugoslavia by Robert Adam in the 18th century.

THE SOHO INN in New Road, Studley, is a popular hostelry. Filled paninis, jacket potatoes, baguettes, and a variety of home-cooked main meals, including a traditional Sunday roast, await the hungry walker. The inn also offers a conservatory and dining area. Wadworth 6X and Henrys IPA are the real ales on offer.
  ✆ 01249 812408.

How to get there: Follow the A4 between Calne and Chippenham and the Soho Inn is on the right as you head west.
Parking: There is room to park at the inn.
Length of the walk: 7 miles. Map: OS Explorer 156 Chippenham & Bradford-on-Avon (GR 971711).

THE WALK

1 From the pub, turn left and follow the pavement beside the A4. Pass the entrance to **Bowood Sports Ground** and the exit road for **Bowood House** and continue under a bridge spanning the road. Turn immediately right beyond it and follow the track to the remains of **Black Dog Halt**. Turn left and follow the disused track bed, part of the old Calne to Chippenham railway, down to a cattle grid and a gate. Leave the old railway at this point to follow a broad path, passing alongside the **River Marden**. Go through the next gate, cross the river and the parallel **Wilts and Berks Canal** and turn right. As you approach **Calne**, keep over to the right and cross several bridges to reach the A4.

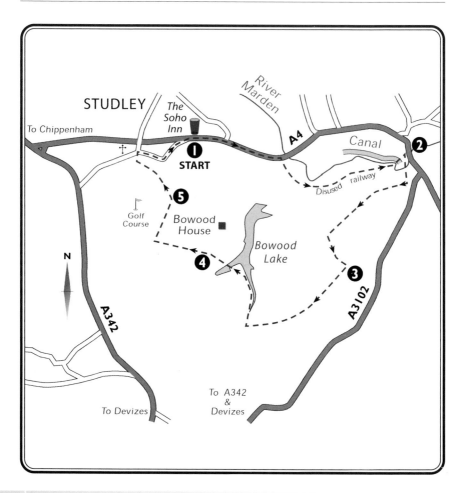

2 *To visit **Calne** turn left here;* to continue the walk turn right into **Station Road** and as it bends right by the fire station, go straight on up a path running between walls and wooden panel fencing. When you reach a lane at the top, turn right and follow it between houses. Soon you reach the edge of **Calne** and now the walk cuts across open country. Trees and rolling farmland line the track now. Descend a slope, climb the other side and take a path on the left, running along the edge of a field. After about 100 yards, climb the bank on the right, bear left and follow the path along the top. Cross a footbridge to a stile in the far boundary, continue ahead to the next waymark and bear left here to a stile. Veer right in the field and follow the path towards a bungalow. On reaching a stile and gate, turn left to follow the drive through the **Bowood estate**. Pass through light woodland to a junction and swing sharp right here.

3 Follow the drive and on the right are glimpses of **Bowood House** in the distance. As you approach a bridge and a lodge beyond it, go through a wrought-iron kissing-gate on the right and follow the meadow along to a bridge. Cross it and follow the path round to the right, keeping the ornamental lake also on the right. Bowood House is clearly seen ahead. As you approach an arm of the lake, veer over to the left and look for a wrought-iron kissing-gate in the fence. With water to the left and right of you, make for the next gate and on the left there is a sign for what is known as the **Store Pool**. Walk ahead up the track, following it as it bends left. Glance back at this point for an excellent view of the estate. At the next junction, avoid the tarmac drive on the extreme right and cross over to a kissing-gate with a waymark.

4 Keep ahead in the field, with the fence on your right, for about 75 yards and bear left at the next waymark. Cross the field, making for a small plantation, and pass through the gate just to the left of it. Keep ahead to the far boundary and exit to a tarmac drive. The fairways of **Bowood Golf Club** can be seen opposite. Turn right and follow the drive round several bends before reaching a sharp right bend by a large mirror for motorists. Go straight on into the trees and then round to the right here, following the path through woodland.

5 On reaching some barns, bear left and head down through the trees to a junction, keeping in line with telephone wires. Keep left and follow the path as it climbs through the woods, with fairways on the left. The main drive to **Bowood** is seen on the right. When you come to a gap in the holly bushes and trees, turn right to the white gates and the road. Turn immediately right into **Old Road** and follow it along to the junction with the A4. Almost opposite is the pub where the walk began.

PLACES OF INTEREST NEARBY

Bowood House and Gardens are well worth a visit after the walk. As well as the house, which includes collections of heirlooms, porcelain and paintings, there are terraced gardens and a lake. Bowood also has a gift shop, a garden centre, a licensed restaurant and a tearoom. Telephone: 01249 812102.

The Royal Oak

STARTING IN THE PICTURESQUE VILLAGE OF WOOTTON RIVERS, THE WALK FOLLOWS THE KENNET & AVON CANAL EAST TOWARDS BURBAGE BEFORE DEPARTING FROM THE WATERWAY TO EXPLORE SOME CLASSIC TRACTS OF UNDULATING, TYPICALLY ENGLISH COUNTRYSIDE.

◆●◆

The design of Wootton Rivers church clock dates back to 1911 and is the brainchild of one Jack Spratt, a colourful local character who, among other things, was an amateur clockmaker. To commemorate the coronation of George V, Wootton Rivers decided to make a clock for the church. However, there were no funds to pay for it so Spratt offered a solution. He would make the clock for nothing, using items of scrap iron, steel, brass and lead.

THE ROYAL OAK is a 16th-century thatched and timbered inn which attracts plenty of summertime walkers. Inside is a wealth of beams and plenty of quaint features. The menu is imaginative and wide-ranging, with an endless choice of starters, main courses and fish dishes. Expect to find Thai chicken curry, lamb cutlets grilled with fresh rosemary, and sauté of calves' liver with bacon and mushrooms. Various lighter meals and lunchtime snacks are also available. Wadworth 6X and a range of guest beers feature among the real ales.
✆ 01672 810322.

How to get there: From Marlborough, take the A346 south towards Burbage. Turn off to the right for Wootton Rivers. The pub is in the main street.
Parking: There is room to park at the Royal Oak or in the village car park in the centre of Wootton Rivers.
Length of the walk: 3 miles. Map: OS Explorer 157 Marlborough & Savernake Forest (GR 196631).

THE WALK

1 From the public car park in the village, turn right and pass the entrance to **St Andrew's church**. Continue along the village street to reach the **Kennet & Avon Canal**, passing the entrance to **Manor Farm** on the way. Cross the canal via the carriage bridge – number 107 – and join the towpath, keeping the canal on your left. Pass **Heathy Close Lock** and head for bridge number 106. Cross the road at this point, noting a large house with tile-hung elevations on the right and a farm on the left. Keep ahead on the towpath to reach **Brimslade Lock**, which forms part of the **Wootton Rivers flight**. Continue beside the canal to the next bridge and leave the towpath at this point.

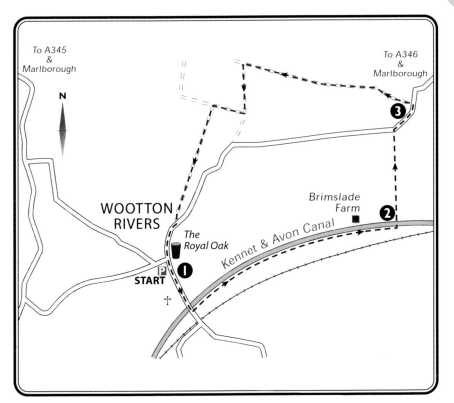

WOOTTON
RIVERS

The
Royal Oak

Brimslade
Farm

Kennet & Avon Canal

START

2 Cross the **Kennet & Avon** and follow the lane, merging with an access road to **Brimslade Farm**. Go straight on up the hill, avoiding a path on the right. Keep on the farm road and at the next junction, bear right. Continue on up the hill and make for a bridleway on the left-hand side of the road, just before the remains of two disused railways. One of them was a branch line serving pupils and staff at nearby **Marlborough College**. Services were in operation until the 1960s.

3 Follow the bridlepath and, at length, you pass a broad opening into a field on the left. Just beyond it is a path junction. Turn left at this stage of the walk and follow the path down to two gateways – one on the left, the other on the right. Pass through the opening on the right, then turn left and follow the field boundary. Bend right in the field corner and continue alongside lines of trees. Head for a wide gateway and a waymark in the perimeter, turn left and descend between trees and hedges. Soon the buildings of **Wootton Rivers** loom into view. Make for the road and veer right to follow it through the village. The **Royal Oak** is reached on the left.

PLACES OF INTEREST NEARBY

Wilton Windmill, near Great Bedwyn, is famous for being the oldest working windmill in Wessex. It was originally constructed in 1821, following the loss of five local windmills when the Kennet & Avon Canal was built. Restored in the 1960s, the windmill is usually open between 2 pm and 5 pm on Sunday and Bank Holiday afternoons between Easter and September. Parties are welcome at other times by arrangement. Telephone: 01672 870202.

The Bell

T HIS DELIGHTFUL WALK FOLLOWS THE BANKS OF THE RIVER KENNET, A POPULAR HAUNT OF WILDLIFE. IN SPRINGTIME BLACK SWANS MAY BE SEEN ON THE RIVER, AND CANADA AND BRENT GEESE ALSO NEST HERE. THE ROUTE CROSSES THE GROUNDS OF LITTLECOTE PARK, PASSING RIGHT ALONGSIDE THE MAGNIFICENT MANSION.

Between AD 908 and 1058, Ramsbury was a bishopric. Today, it is a large village, popular with locals and city commuters. One of its most famous features, the huge hollow elm, is still fondly remembered in Ramsbury. Situated in the village square, it had to be cut down in the 1980s and was replaced by an oak tree. Built between 1490 and 1520 and used as the headquarters of the 101st Airborne Division during the Second World War, nearby Littlecote House is supposedly where Henry VIII courted Jane Seymour.

THE BELL is a 300-year-old former coaching inn standing at the very heart of Ramsbury, overlooking the village square. The varied menu changes on a regular basis but old favourites tend to include Ramsbury ale and local beef pie and a range of fresh fish dishes. Sandwiches and ploughman's lunches are also available. Beers include Ramsbury Gold and Pophams Pride. There is no food on Sunday evening. This popular hostelry has been the subject of an extensive refurbishment programme in recent years.
✆ 01672 520230.

How to get there: Ramsbury is east of Marlborough. From the town you can cut across country through Mildenhall and Axford. From Swindon or Hungerford follow the B4192 and turn off at the Ramsbury sign.
Parking: There is a car park at the pub.
Length of the walk: 5 miles. Map: OS Explorer 157 Marlborough & Savernake Forest; 158 Newbury & Hungerford (GR 276716).

THE WALK

1 From the pub car park in the centre of **Ramsbury**, turn left and follow **Scholards Lane**. When the road changes name to become **The Knap**, turn right at the sign for **Froxfield**. Cross the meandering **River Kennet** – broad and shallow here – and walk along to the point where a right of way crosses the road. Turn left for **Littlecote**, ignore a bridleway on the right and continue ahead on the track. This stage of the circuit heralds the start of

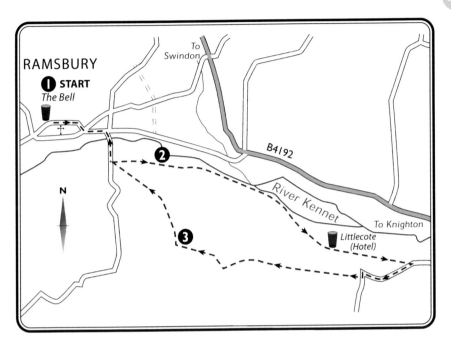

a lengthy stretch of walking with the Kennet for company and few signs of civilization.

2 Pass a brick cottage with a circular addition – it may well have once been a dovecote – and keep the property's riverside garden over to your left. Keep ahead along the left-hand edge of farmland and eventually the outline of **Littlecote House** peeps into view across sprawling parkland. Continue walking towards the house and, when you draw level with wrought-iron gates, keep ahead along an avenue of lime trees to reach the road. Turn right and when the lane bends sharp left, keep ahead to a gate. At this point the walk re-enters the grounds of **Littlecote**. At the bend, by a 'way out' sign, follow the stony track ahead. Ignore a track running off sharp right and pass a line of ancient beech trees to reach a fork. Veer right and follow one of the old concrete tracks that originally formed part of a wartime airfield here.

3 At the next waymarked intersection keep right and head up the slope through the trees. At the point where the track sweeps to the right, continue straight ahead along the obvious woodland path. Keep to the path as it descends quite steeply, pass a conveniently placed seat on the right and head in the direction of **Ramsbury**. On reaching the next junction bear left to the road, turn right and retrace your steps back to **Ramsbury**.

PLACES OF INTEREST NEARBY

Littlecote House is now a hotel but if you do this glorious walk on a Sunday, you'll find the house is open to the public all day. The haunted bedroom where a mother and her baby are said to have been murdered and the Long Gallery are well worth a look and even today a ghostly atmosphere pervades the place. Telephone: 01488 682509.

The Inn with the Well

THIS SPECTACULAR WALK IS IN TYPICAL WILTSHIRE DOWNLAND COUNTRY, MUCH OF IT FAR REMOVED FROM SIGNS OF CIVILISATION, ROADS, HOUSES AND THE USUAL REMINDERS OF MODERN LIFE. ALMOST IMMEDIATELY, IT CLIMBS HIGH ABOVE THE VILLAGE OF OGBOURNE ST GEORGE, AT LENGTH DISAPPEARING INTO AN ENCLOSED LAND OF BARE HILLS AND WOODS. THE FINAL STAGE OF THE WALK IS ALONG THE RIDGEWAY, A ROUTE OF GREAT ANTIQUITY.

Now a long-distance footpath, the Ridgeway was originally a major east–west route in prehistoric Britain. From this high ground there are magnificent views across to Barbury Castle. This is an Iron Age hill fort of about 12 acres. The site is named after Bera, a tribal chief. Wiltshire County Council has created a popular country park here.

The **INN WITH THE WELL**, formerly the Old Crown, is a warm, friendly inn that is popular with local walkers and hikers undertaking the nearby Ridgeway. An 18th-century freehouse with a floodlit well, the inn offers Ridgeway trampers a perfect excuse to stop for refreshment. The pub takes its name from the well set in the restaurant floor. Reinforced glass allows customers to stand on top and peer inside.

Three real ales are sourced from micro and regional brewers and there is a good choice of snacks and main meals. The inn is closed at lunchtime on Monday to Thursday (inclusive) between November and March.

✆ 01672 841335.

How to get there: Ogbourne St George is between Marlborough and Swindon, just off the A346. The Inn with the Well is in the village centre.

Parking: There is usually room to park at the pub. If not, there may be some spaces in the main street or along the road almost opposite the inn.

Length of the walk: 4½ miles. Map: OS Explorer 157 Marlborough and Savernake Forest (GR 203742).

THE WALK

1 Turn right, out of the car park, and pass beneath the A346 flyover. Bear right signposted 'Bytham Farm'. Walk along the lane – part of a Roman road. The main road and the disused **Midland South-West Junction railway** are just a few yards away on the right. Glancing over to the westerly horizon, you will spot the outline of **Barbury Castle**. Go past a cottage and on reaching a sign '**Auto Plant Services**', bear left and proceed up the track.

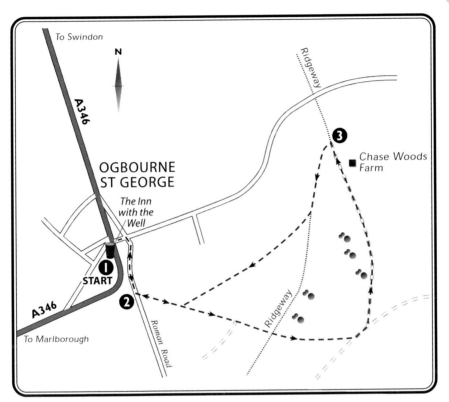

2 Pass the light industrial plant on the right. Beyond it carry on up the track between hedgerows. Further up, it is worth pausing to look back for a spectacular view over to **Barbury Castle**, with **Ogbourne St George** in the foreground. At the top of the hill merge with the **Ridgeway** and follow it for a short distance until you reach a junction of tracks. Ignore left and right turnings and keep ahead. Pass a large house on the left, which is a tasteful conversion from the sundry farm buildings which previously occupied the site. This stretch of the walk provides distant glimpses of the downland country where it reaches down to the **Kennet valley**. The track makes a gradual descent. Pass a turning on the left down to a farm and continue between lines of trees.

Soon you merge with another track. Bear left, ignoring the track ahead. After several minutes you reach a fork. Take the left-hand track, ignoring the turning to **Stock Lane**. Keep on the track as it cuts between fields and bursts of woodland. Eventually, you come up to some barns, various old farm buildings and cottages. Go over a cattle grid and pass the entrance to a solitary house on the edge of the trees over to the right. Pass over another grid and continue beyond several more houses.

3 Take the sharp left-hand track, rejoining the **Ridgeway**, and follow it between trees and hedgerows. There are good downland views to the right. From here you can spot traffic on the main A346. The **Ridgeway** tends to be wide in places, as when the original line became weathered or difficult to negotiate, the traveller moved to one side and so made the track wider. After several minutes or so, look for a path on the right. It runs down the slope, cutting between fences and hedgerows. Take the path and follow it, with excellent views of **Ogbourne St George**, and **Barbury Castle** rising above it. Keep on the path, with clear uninterrupted views. Further down, the path joins the track you came up at the start of the walk. Follow it down the hill, turn right at the junction and, at the road junction, bear left to the pub car park.

PLACES OF INTEREST NEARBY

For a great day out for all the family, visit the **Steam Museum** of the Great Western Railway at Swindon. Here is the chance to learn all about the GWR through imaginative displays and hands-on exhibitions. You can even get on the footplate and experience what it was like to be a train driver during the great days of steam. Find out, too, about the company's engineering genius – Isambard Kingdom Brunel. Telephone: 01793 466646.

The Shepherd's Rest

THE GLORIOUS WIDE OPEN SPACES OF WILTSHIRE, THE SENSE OF HISTORY AND FREEDOM, AND THE TIMELESS APPEAL OF THAT PREHISTORIC ROUTE KNOWN AS THE RIDGEWAY ARE ALL PERFECTLY REFLECTED IN THIS WALK ACROSS THE NORTH WESSEX DOWNS. THE RETURN LEG IS VIA TWO PRETTY VILLAGES, BISHOPSTONE AND HINTON PARVA, WITH SOME ROAD WALKING ALONG QUIET LANES. STRINGS OF HORSES MAY BE SEEN FROM TIME TO TIME ON THE ROUTE.

The downs rise to 800 ft as you join the Ridgeway, now one of the Countryside Commission's national trails, stretching for 85 miles between Avebury and Ivinghoe Beacon. Our route covers only about a mile of it but the feeling of peace and tranquillity on these downs is second to none.

THE SHEPHERD'S REST is a quaint old Flowers inn with the distinction of being the only pub directly on the route of the Ridgeway. Originally, it was favoured by drovers and shepherds

who used the route to transport their cattle and sheep. It is the inn's position on one of Britain's most popular national trails that has helped to establish the Shepherd's Rest as a local landmark and a noted hostelry with a warm, friendly atmosphere. The food available includes bison burgers, venison and other game dishes. Shepherd Neame Spitfire is among the real ales on offer.
✆ 01793 790266.

How to get there: Follow the B4192 between Hungerford and Swindon and, on the stretch between Aldbourne and Liddington, turn off at the sign for Baydon and Hinton Parva, a few yards from the point where the road crosses the M4. Follow the road to Fox Hill and the pub is at the crossroads.

Parking: There is room to park at the front and side of the inn and there is also a large layby nearby.

Length of the walk: 4½ miles. Map: OS Explorer 170 Abingdon and Vale of White Horse (GR 231814).

THE WALK

① From the front of the inn bear left to the crossroads, then left again heading towards **Hinton Parva** and **Bishopstone**. When the road curves left after about 150 yards, leave it and join the unmetalled **Ridgeway**, signposted 'Wayland's Smithy, Uffington Castle and Streatley'. The path begins a gradual ascent to climb up between **Charlbury Hill** and **Fox Hill** with the outline of a transmitter on the hilltop on the right. Pass the route of a bridleway and press on over this breezy ground. On the left are grand views over north Wiltshire towards the **Vale of the White Horse**. Ignore a turning on the left and continue.

Further on, there are glorious views stretching to the horizon. On a good day the cooling towers of **Didcot power station** are visible. The **Ridgeway** begins to descend between hedgerows. Keep on the main path and when it levels out, at a staggered

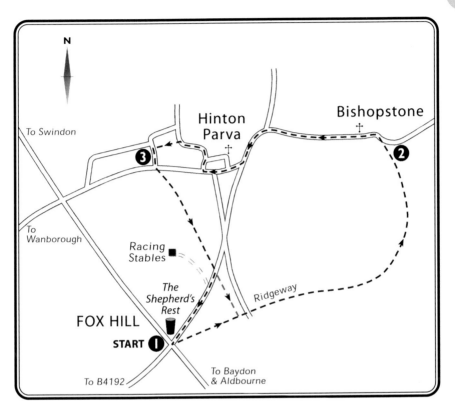

crossroads, bear left through a gate to join a waymarked bridleway. Aim for a fold in the coombe ahead and follow the bridleway. Go through a gate and across the centre of a large field to a pair of kissing-gates. Be sure to take the left gate which joins a track. A little later the track swings left between hedgerows. Eventually, you reach the road.

2 Turn left and walk through the village of **Bishopstone**. The church may be glimpsed on the right. Head out of the village and follow the road between fields. At the junction veer left, signposted '**Wanborough**'. After a short distance look for a stile and some railings in the bank on the right. Cross into the field and go forward to the far boundary. Pass through a kissing-gate and proceed ahead to the next boundary. Here you negotiate another kissing-gate beside a wrought-iron gate. Go forward along a path. Note the churchyard on your right. At the road, in the centre of the pretty village of **Hinton Parva**, turn right and after a few yards bear right again opposite some thatched cottages. Follow the road round the left bend and on the next bend leave the road and follow the footpath, signposted 'The Grove', down to a kissing-gate. Go along a straight path beyond, cutting between fields. At the road turn left and in a couple of minutes or so you reach another junction.

(3) Cross over at this point and follow the waymarked bridleway running alongside the village hall. Further on, it narrows to a path and climbs gradually high above the fields and downland. Looking back, there are very good views to the north, with the houses of **Hinton Parva** in the foreground. This area is managed by the National Trust and is known as 'The Coombes'. Pass through a gate and continue, crossing the all-weather training gallops. The buildings of **Stan Mellor's racing stables** come into view on the right. The yard is named **Badgerstown**, after a noted racehorse of recent times. On reaching the road you have a choice. To avoid any more road walking, continue over the road and along the next stretch of bridleway until you reach the **Ridgeway**. Turn right and follow it back to the inn. Alternatively, return to the **Shepherd's Rest** by bearing right and following the road all the way. It is a relatively quiet lane, so there should be no problems about heavy traffic.

PLACES OF INTEREST NEARBY

The 17th-century **Ashdown House**, owned by the National Trust and situated between Lambourn and Ashbury, conveys the impression of a large-scale doll's house. It looks curiously out of place in its windswept setting on the chalk downs. Telephone: 01793 762209 or the information line on 01494 755569 for more details.